To Marilyn —

Gloria Stern

Do The Write Thing

Making the Transition to Professional

Gloria Stern

Printed and bound in the United States of America. All rights reserved. No part of this book may be reproduced or transmitted in any form or by any means, electronic or mechanical, including photocopying, recording, or by an information storage and retrieval system -- except by a reviewer who may quote brief passages in a review to be printed in a magazine or a newspaper without obtaining permission in writing from the publisher.

Copyright, © 1993 by
GLORIA STERN

MYRIAD PRESS
12535 Chandler Blvd #3
N. Hollywood, CA 91607-1934

Library of Congress Card Number 94-76929

Stern, Gloria
Do The Write Thing/Gloria Stern
Includes Glossary, Appendix and Index
1. Writing, 2. Publishing and Publishers
ISBN 0-9641266-0-5

I shot an >>>>>>>> into the air
It fell to earth I knew not where
    at Random House.
I sent a manuscript proper and stamped
    to Random House.
Got no reply. Was my style cramped?
Definitely not. I sent another
    to Random House.
Still no reply. Is there some other
Person to whom I can appeal
    at Random House?
To be ignored is too unreal.
Are my missives in limbo like my
    >>>>>>>>'s
    at Random House ?
If so this is sent via two trained
    sparrows..... to Random House

Through the courtesy of Samuel Zimberoff

ACKNOWLEDGMENTS:

This is my opportunity to express my deep appreciation to my students at Valley College whose enthusiasm and dedication inspired and energized the creation of this book, to Ann Kempner Fisher for her irreplaceable help and encouragement, to Aiko Schick, proofreader and editor, who so generously gave of her expertise and time and to my children, to Patty, who supported me throughout the long process and lastly, to Stephen, whose timely contribution made all the difference. Many thanks to those special people who helped to bring this book to fruition.

North Hollywood, 1993

TABLE OF CONTENTS

INTRODUCTION..1

CHAPTER ONE

TO DO OR NOT TO DO..5

The creative writer - Breaking into print - Telling a story with a beginning, middle and end - Storytelling from before written history to electronic transmission - The completed manuscript - Taking the plunge: Looking for an agent or publisher - The form response - Becoming your own publisher - A subsidy house - Success models - The mindset of a professional author.

CHAPTER TWO

SCRIBE OR SCRIBBLER...16

Kinds of books that attract a readership - What things a publisher considers - Getting "repped" - Working with a collaborator - Garnering literary credits - The virtuoso writer - Inspiration versus perspiration - Advances, royalties, the contract and the lawyers - The place of the mentor - Rounding up the ghost writers - Your own literary consultant - Working with a partner - Contests and winners.

CHAPTER THREE

THE BUSINESS OF THE BUSINESS...28

Six figure contracts - Keeping the tally - Remainders and returns - Tax laws - The advance - The publisher funds the project - Working against a deadline - Royalties - Unsolicited manuscripts - Your image as a writer - writing credits - Using a pen name - Legitimate business expenses - Incorporating yourself - Responsibilities and obligations - Plagiarism - Authorization - Sponsoring yourself - Opportunities and unexpected pleasures - Working writers and writer's work - Writers' groups - Perceptions of the writer.

CHAPTER FOUR

HIGH RISE STORIES..42

New techniques for communication - CD Rom's and the electronic superhighway - The best formulas, techniques, and writing rules - Writing a life story - A writer-for-hire - Gauging a writer's worth - The plot thickens, permanently - Action/ misadventure - Character vs role - Category fiction - Mainstream novels - Competition - Popular fiction - Fiction/non-fiction - Styles in the media - The first bid for professional status - Patterns in contemporary fiction - Writing about what intrigues, surprises or annoys - Exploiting your writing talent - Subjects and ideas - Objectivity - Classy or classical?

CHAPTER FIVE

THE MARKETPLACE AND THE MANUSCRIPT..................61

The finished and ready to go to market - Destination night-stand - A successful publishing venture - Classifications, - tip sheets and writing to spec - The market is defined - Exactly what it is you have to sell - Strategies you can learn about marketing - Fashions in fiction - Selecting the market before starting the manuscript - Writing from a personal story - Selling your rights - The first novel - Getting to Bestseller lists - Ways to qualify as an experienced author.

CHAPTER SIX

THE COPYRIGHT..76

Ownership of literary property - "Fair use" - Sections 107 through 118 of the Copyright Act - Classes of copyright - Pre-publication registration - Registration after publication - How long does copyright last? - International copyright - Berne convention - Transfer or assignment of statutory copyright - Copyright procedure for published works - Secondary markets - International standard book number - Library of Congress Card catalog number.

CHAPTER SEVEN

THE SQUARE IN THE MIDDLE..90

Getting the book published - Dealing directly with the publisher - The publisher's submissions format - Knowing which publishing house to choose - Reading the contract - Representing yourself: Help, hype and hope - A writer's worth - Recognizing trends in reading - The Boomerang Press - A positive outlook - Gaining some understanding of the publication process - Being a writer's writer.

CHAPTER EIGHT

THE PUBLISHER..103

Big publishing houses and small publishing houses - Self-publication - Taking a book through the publication process - The readers of your book - The function of the book distributor - Publishers' overruns - Creating a bestseller - The back list - Responsibilities and rewards - What does a publisher do ? - Book producers and the way they work - Making an offer they can't refuse - Rights of first refusal - The book publishing contract.

CHAPTER NINE

ON THE WAY TO THE WEDDING..117

Presenting your manuscript for acceptance - Your initial presentation - An ugly duckling is not a swan - Computer generated hard copy - The look of the presentation - Reader identification - Originality, yes or no? Presenting a non-fiction book - Is there a need for copyright - The fiction manuscript - About first novels - Bestseller lists.

CHAPTER TEN

THE AGENT...132

Looking for Mr. Goodwrite - Querying for a career - The cover letter - The synopsis - The writer's bio - Organizing the search - Multiple submissions - When editing is needed - Consultation services, the agency - The book proposal is developed - What to expect from your agent - The agent who is a perfect match for you - A workable union is formed - Negotiations.

CHAPTER ELEVEN

WHAT TO DO UNTIL THE SCRIPT DOCTOR COMES.......143

The "R" word - Those nasty form letters - A wordsmith strikes back - Post graduate grades - Darma drama - Style, trends and dressing write - Myths, fables, parables and allegories - POV; B.M.E; and END - Gunning-Fog Index - Electronic help - Writing is rewriting - Rejections are not forever - Hitting it write on!

GLOSSARY...151

APPENDIX..157

    1. Submission Format
    2. Proposal for Non-fiction
    3. Checklist for Fiction
    4. Sample Cover Letter
    5. Proof Marks
    6. Permissions Letter
    7. Resource Addresses
    8. Items in an Agent/Publisher Contract

INDEX..171

Introduction
****

The creative writing process is a solitary one. The germ of an idea may lie dormant for an indeterminate period, but, eventually, unbidden, it comes to the surface and the stuff held in memory takes on life. Wanting the whole world to share in this unique and extraordinary event, the would-be author quite understandably sets his sights on the day when he will see his work published.

He perseveres through the long isolated process of getting it all down on paper, through the difficult business of writing and rewriting, revision after revision, draft after draft. Knowing that it takes an original theme or unusual point of view to get a book on the shelves of a bookstore, the optimistic writer continues with refining his manuscript long past the time for letting go. Though friends and acquaintances may have read it, lavishing sweet, welcome praise on its creator and from that friendly jury it is unanimously judged ready for the marketplace, no amount of accolades will guarantee its general distribution.

Amateurs write for fun, professionals write for fun and profit. The difference is very obvious. Professionals get paid. No amount of generous friends can properly compensate a writer for his efforts. To become a professional requires that someone accept the manuscript for publication and produce a book for the reading and buying public.

Making the decision to get published is the turning point in a writer's career. The transition demands a good deal of new knowledge. Because necessary information is so replete and varied, it is not easy to find. As questions begin to arise the writer starts a whirlwind of investigation scurrying around from place to place, from reference book to reference book.

Each newfound answer brings up additional questions. Usual first time worries, such as: "How can I protect my ideas?" and, "Should I pay a reader's fee?" turn out to be frivolous concerns which waste time and delay the process.

Until he actually begins the task, the new professional has no idea which questions to ask. He struggles with others, only slightly more meaningful, like: "Can I submit computer generated copy? - or is a floppy disk okay?". "When do I need to copyright my material?" And, if so, "How do I go about it?" "Where should my manuscript be sent?" and, "To whom?", "Should I use an agent or work directly with a publisher?" Soon he wants to know: "Is it to my advantage to register myself as a business?"; "Under what circumstances do I use a nom de plume?" Without help, finding the answers becomes a complex, confusing and time consuming task.

Inventing the solutions for some and ignoring others, the anxious author begins the job of seeking a publisher. Carefully bound and posted (along with the hopes of its creator), the script embarks on the project's most significant phase; it is proudly offered a potential public. The writer places it in the mail only to see his creation returned to the point of origin like an unerring boomerang to remain in the cursed condition of an unsold, unagented and, by definition, an unprofessional manuscript.

All of the above mentioned questions and concerns are answered in this book, along with more weighty considerations, such as: "What does a professional writer need to know about the publishing business?" And, "What do agents look for in a manuscript?" And that constant nagging quandary, "How long should I wait before beginning a follow up?"

After sending it out to publisher after publisher and having it repeatedly returned, its creator, by now, has suffered the twin pains of embarrassment and frustration resulting from numerous unexplained rejections. He/she is forced to face an ongoing process that is an unfathomable mystery with not a clue as to what to do about it which is why I have included a special feature in the final chapter that can be found nowhere else...a subject that every writer faces but no one talks about -- what to do about repeated rejections.

The aspiring but untutored writer grudgingly goes through the painful process of learning that by simply having written a truly original piece, his effort does not necessarily produce offers for publication. At this point, he wonders whether his work is even worthy. For some, this, then, becomes the sad ending to what was once a vision of recognition, remuneration or even personal fame. The effort dies here, lovingly remembered, but gone, the victim of a perplexing system.

In my capacity as an independent literary agent, I deal with submissions every day. It's my job. I know the answers to the puzzle. I know that only <u>two percent</u> of manuscripts submitted do not require additional editing or revision.

For any writer who has ever wondered why his work was rejected, there is a unique section on just that very topic, one I have never seen addressed anywhere else. Happily, the chapter spells out suggestions, that, if followed, will give the author a definite edge.

When I was offered the opportunity to teach what I know about manuscript submissions in a structured situation, I was delighted. In the course of developing a syllabus, I was surprised to learn that there is no one authoritative, concise, reader-friendly publication containing all the relevant information needed for the process. The necessary information is scattered in a great many locations. Just finding it takes research, persistence, know-how and wit (and mistakes and rejections can be costly) and if the search is not successful, they can rob one of enthusiasm and hope. (One non-writer who told me his supposed method for finding a publisher, quipped, "You just keep knocking on doors until you find one." But then, he never tried.)

When I began teaching the course, my students asked all manner of questions about how they could make the transition to professional. Inspired by their enthusiasm and aided by their questions, I compiled this definitive handbook, "a one-stop shopping" source containing the steps, guidelines and answers they needed. I knew I had something that could change those discouraging two percent statistics into hopes for career success for many aspiring authors. It is in that spirit that I wrote this book.

Chapter One
****

TO DO OR NOT TO DO

> Breathes there a man with head so dead
> Who never to himself hath said,
> "I have this great idea for a TV series..."
>
>   (with apologies to Sir Walter Scott)

If you substitute the words "sit-com"; novel"; "film"; "drama"; "stand-up comedy routine", or any of your choice of narrative presentations, almost everyone will have heard that familiar bluster at least once. Is there anyone who has not heard some such casual remark spoken at a party, a football game, or perhaps at a bus stop or even while waiting in line to purchase a theater ticket?

Reviewers and critics hear the boast with unbelievable frequency, but literary agents know that there is a vast difference between the idea of breaking into print and the actual accomplishment. It is appreciably easier to fantasize the wonders of an imaginary story, but it is not until all the problems of structure, characterization, story line and pacing have been worked out that the reality of making it happen becomes realized. The conversion of an idea into a manuscript produces a comparable transformation in the viewpoint of the author as he stands ready to join those who "put the pen to paper".

Each of us is a unique person with an original background and pool of individual experiences. We have different skills and talents. Many of us will have had singular experiences we wish to share. The urge for self expression and the need to seek community is basic to human nature. The urge to tell a story is both universal and ageless. Even when daily activity brings one in close contact with others, as a means of communication, writing a book has a very special purpose fueled by potent human drives; for the telling of a story with a beginning, middle and end fills a primal need in man, the need to make sense of experience and produce order from the chaos of living. Joseph L. Mankiewicz, when speaking about his special field of creativity expressed it well when he said, "The difference between life and the movies is that a script has to make sense, and life doesn't." To originate a book is a prestigious and satisfying aspiration, one with which we can all identify, and to which we are all qualified in varied measure, for each of us has within him something distinctive and original to relate to the world and by sharing it with others, add to the reasonableness of life. A book opens the door to perception allowing the reader to enter new and distant worlds. It is an achievement that makes man greater than he is and brings him closer to the gods.

Storytelling dates back well before written history. Even before pictographs and hieroglyphics there was the sacred tradition of oral history. When man began to grunt intelligibly, he told his fellow tribesman of dangers and delights in his daily adventures. Social and spiritual life centered around oral tradition. With the advent of the printing press and the growth of literacy, the written word became the method of choice by which information could be transmitted. Even in our high tech world, the universal acceptance of electronic transmission of data does not take the place of the necessity for, or the desire for, written communication and the development of narrative skills.

That need to validate personal experience by sharing it is a natural drive in all of us but undeveloped in some and dormant in others. Though this possibility exists in the minds of many, more than a few manage to see that goal realized. Some writers live with the thought of a book ever present in the back of their minds. Others, more skilled or more motivated, actually proceed to put their unique collection of information into the form of a manuscript. Last year, 60,000 volumes were printed, released and distributed. Add to that number the thousands of manuscripts that never were registered, plus the hundreds of thousands of authors still in the process of working on autobiographies, biographies, both authorized and unauthorized; war memoirs, children's stories, how-to's, self help texts, new age, old age, babies, mothers, mothers who work, health and beauty, cook books, romance novels, sci-fi, true crime and humor -- not forgetting the high numbers of mainstream novels in process.

MAKING THE DECISION

Whether writing a book is, as yet, a vague yearning or a present concrete reality, everyone who dreams of a career as a writer can identify with the task. Having made the decision to create, there is research, structure, format and transcript to master. Once you've taken the courses, attended the seminars, and listened to the lectures and persuaded yourself that the manuscript is not only readable, but probably better than you would have thought. (Can I tell you how many times I've heard the phrase "better than most of the stuff that's out there" ?), you make the commitment to yourself to see what can be done about getting it published.

After having spent long lonely hours in research, at the library or at the work desk and taking the manuscript though countless rewrites, the enthusiastic author becomes convinced that he has created a fine project that is now worthy of the marketplace. With determination, he declares that, "The last rewrite was the last it's going to get." Proudly he proclaims the manuscript completed. All that is needed now is the proper exposure. His work is ready to send out into the world, hopefully to be put into the hands of millions of readers waiting to read the precious oeurve. Undoubtedly, a good idea is the prerequisite to getting any story into print, but between the good idea and the public lies production, publication, distribution and/or performance.

DEALING WITH THE BOOMERANG PRESS

Most writers starting the process toward getting into print usually begin by attempting to contact an agent or a publisher though an associate even on their own. The high profile celebrity may have his manager or his lawyer make the connection for him. As for John Doe, ordinary citizen, his path is not so simple. If the would-be author is one of the principals in a notable event, he may be lucky enough to find there is a ready made demand for his story. He may even be approached for his version, or, in the case of the inexperienced writer, the approach may include the offer of a ghost writer. First novelists who persevere through to publication are rare; the path is perilous and they often find that without assistance, verging on impossible.

Even the most prestigious of publishing houses will extend the offer to purchase to fewer than ten authors in a single year and, as a rule, only through the recommendation of someone with whom they have worked with before. These privileged few may come highly recommended by an astute agent, from an academic mentor or from a bestselling author who is already earning large sums of money for the publisher. One or two of this special class of novice writers may be gloriously successful in achieving high selling volume, an achievement which places his name on the "A" list forever, remaining as an inspiration and incentive to others to try. For those who are not so blessed, the dogeared manuscript is returned (provided you have included return postage) with a form letter reading:

> Thank you for sending your manuscript to us for our examination. Unfortunately, we do not feel it meets our current list. However, be assured, we wish you luck with it elsewhere.

Occasionally, if the reader is sympathetic and someone who has an understanding of the plight of the creative individual, he will write:

> The rejection of a manuscript does not necessarily indicate inadequate ideas or ability. It simply means that the volume does not fit into our current search for appropriate material for our list. Also, it should be mentioned that we may have already purchased a similar idea, and we cannot use a second.

Some of the less stalwart new authors find such impersonal replies discouraging. Note that this state of affairs is the norm and to be expected. The purchase of a book manuscript is a step never taken without the enthusiastic endorsement of the marketing, advertising, and production departments and is not necessarily due to the content or quality of the submission.

MAKING BOOK -- (YOURS)

If he has been plagued by a number of unsuccessful submissions, the unhappy writer contemplates a rewrite at some later date. Before abandoning his creation to obscurity he faces three alternatives. He either puts the script aside for a while to formulate a new plan, chucks it entirely or determines to publish it himself.

The third alternative brings up the problem of learning what self-publication is all about. Start by asking yourself whether you have the strong entrepreneurial spirit needed to begin a new endeavor. Determination and energy are required to see the project to completion and while it is a very rewarding task, it does not hold many of the benefits that go along with major publishing house sponsorship. A job of this magnitude takes a special set of attributes; decisiveness, a willingness to talk about yourself publicly, and the ability to persevere alone through a myriad of unfamiliar decisions.

It is certainly possible to self-publish, however it is one option that should be carefully considered. It is a costly procedure. The first step is to have a firm idea of what you want the book to look like. In order for that vision to be realized it takes special talent, training and experience. The process of self-publication requires engaging a graphic artist to create the design for the book's graphics, together you must choose the suitable fonts, gather the illustrations and charts, paginate, concoct chapter headings, prepare a table of contents and an index if needed, and you will want to have an attractive cover created for the book, as well. Someone will need to originate a subtitle and write the copy for the back cover. Furthermore, there is the matter of copyright registration and it is necessary to obtain an ISBN (International Standard Book

Number) and a Library of Congress number, too. (More about this later.) All these tasks are specific and require specialized knowledge. Besides, they take time and energy away from writing.

Once those decisions are made, there are additional jobs to perform. A printer needs to be hired. An arrangement has to be made with a storage facility (also known as a fulfillment house) to warehouse all those thousands of books while waiting for the orders to roll in. Then the orders have to be efficiently processed. A fulfillment house needs to be located for this process and a contract draw up. Advertising and book reviews come next. You can't sell a book if the public doesn't know it's there so you write to talk shows and church and school program producers. If the rent on the storage facility starts to mount up, you might consider hiring a PR person to arrange book signings and public appearances to help you generate sales or book yourself in the media and issue press releases.

Being your own publisher entails a financial risk. Even though the percentage of return is higher when you publish yourself, the number of books sold, for the most part, may not be equal to that of a major publisher who has in his circle of associates overseas representatives and agents who have access to auxiliary markets.

All this is a time consuming effort; one that didn't really come as a happily anticipated task in the first flush of inspiration and one that is apt to become increasingly frustrating as the relevant facts become more and more apparent.

The president of one of the preeminent subsidy houses acknowledges that only one out of twenty-five of the authors' works he publishes makes money. (Of course, there may be other reasons for self publishing besides profit, though they apply mostly to a non-fiction book written by an author who is already engaged in dealing with the public.) If you find the thought of keeping track of book store placement, bookkeeping, storage and shipping more than you are willing to undertake, there are several reliable distribution companies which can serve your needs.

DO IT YOURSELF HIGH TECH

The technological advances of production techniques have elevated self-publishing to new standards with good looking pages, glossy attractive covers and artistic graphics. It is something to consider before giving up entirely on publication and allowing the manuscript to gather dust.

A whole new industry has been created with the advent of desktop publishing. Computer generated data flows out fully ready to be turned over to the printer, who then prepares the copy for the press. Pictures, graphs and charts can be created at home in quiet and privacy. Elaborate pictorials may require more memory. Since a complete book can be written on a 100 Mb hard drive, using home computers to create all manner of printed material becomes possible for many more people. Publication falls within the capabilities of almost everyone. Undoubtedly, PC disks are the writer's tools of the future.

In conjunction with this development is the potential for a new market, the creation, sale and distribution of a manuscript through the electronic superhighway. Companies have been established offering catalogues via electronic addresses. It is simple to have your book included in one of these listings.

VANITY PRESS

If the complexities of self-publishing are too much trouble, the perplexed author might try publication with a vanity press which will print any book at the expense of the author. Charges to the writer include printing and binding, storage and the services of the fulfillment house. Though this process, all of these costs fall to the impoverished but satisfied writer who will then have the joyous satisfaction of seeing his words in print and knowing that the time spent creating it was not in vain.

If this alternative is his choice, the aspiring author can have the relief of avoiding the always time consuming process of submitting his material pondering the possibility of receiving a carefully worded rejection letter. Some of the more tedious chores of self publication can be eliminated entirely if one of any number of these subsidy presses is selected.

Frequently, as a consequence, the author-creator is left with a garage filled with volumes should he be unable to secure a distributor. However, the subsidy press option, if conducted properly by someone with a following, can generate a high profit margin and be commercially successful, especially if the author is able to generate his own market by holding seminars, appearing on talk shows and advertising in trade journals. Self-publishing is especially useful if money is not the only motive for publication. Book sales are a valuable adjunct to promote a person already in the public eye. Public speakers benefit from the method. Occasionally, the success of a self-published volume will attract a publisher with national distribution and advertising.

One impressive model of success is the occupational guide, "What Color Is Your Parachute?". Richard Nelson

Bolles sold the rights to the self-published text to the Ten Speed Press which puts out a new edition yearly attracting an ever larger market. Another spectacular effort "The One Minute Manager" by Kenneth Blanchard, Ph.D., and Spencer Johnson, M.D. which was originally a self-published book was purchased by Berkeley Publishing Group to garner fantastic sales.

However, if the dream for seeing the manuscript on book shelves in stores everywhere is very strong and the vision of fame and glory includes commercial success and the validation demonstrated by profit-making potential, you will want to have the benefit of experts to aid you in your journey to becoming a professional author.

In order for this to occur, the manuscript must be sold to the publishing house that will best perform the job of taking your manuscript, editing it, designing it, creating their own copyright, printing it, distributing it and assuming the awesome responsibility for developing the market in order for it to reach the reading public. This takes experienced personnel and the system to activate the plan. While all this is taking place, the author is obliged to develop an inordinate amount of cooperation and trust.

PUTTING THE WORD(S) OUT

Manuscripts come in many shapes and formats. There are text books and storytelling books, manuals and workbooks, cookbooks and children's books, mysteries and books about current events and famous people, but unless the text is written expressly for a private journal, no matter what the topic or the treatment, the words are meant for circulation and intended to be read. For it to be read by its targeted readership, the manuscript must be transformed from its format as a personal document into a volume appropriate for public acceptance. Along with that evolution is the accompanying transformation of its creator from amateur to professional, a very special journey reserved for a dedicated class of people.

Chapter Two

SCRIBE OR SCRIBBLER

> I write, not because I want to, but because I have to. The only balm for this obsession is, that hopefully, the practice is forcing an improvement in my output.
> - G. Stern

In my work as a literary consultant I frequently hear some version of the sentiment expressed in the quote above. To me it signals the beginning of what I call the "buckle up and buckle down" phase, an identifiable period in the making of any writer. It denotes the willingness of the author to focus on improving his craft above any unrealistic fantasies of easy fame and fortune he may harbor.

The creative writer is a very special sort of person. He endures a great deal of voluntary solitude, throughout which he maintains a singular individualism. His vision guides his life and his spirit fuels his work. In the world he creates, the characters are his principal companions. His joy, as well as his pain, is found in his work.

Many people, if questioned, would probably assume that the story is what sells a book. If that were so, there would be many more books published. The story is only of prime importance if the book is based on reporting where accuracy gives the document its value. For each classification a different element is needed. For self-help, personal testimony in the form of vignettes and case histories add veracity. While style and content are fundamental factors in the decision whether or not to accept a manuscript for publication, they are not the only factors. A dynamic narrative told in a spellbinding style certainly goes a long way toward convincing the powers that be that the project ought to be considered, but the decision will not be implemented before some other very rudimentary elements are taken into account. The product cannot be viewed apart from its creator.

For books to attract a sizable readership, one that will produce profits for the author, the designer, the printer, the distributor and the book store owner, it is essential that the publication be brought to the attention of the buying public. Book producers, aware of this need, look for something extra in the campaign to create popular demand. Some of these advantages might be: the name and picture of a high profile person on the jacket, an dynamite expose of a recent historical event, a controversial topic currently in the media or a new volume from the pen of a writer who has previously demonstrated success. It sounds like a catch 22, and it prompts the question "How do you get to be a professional writer if no one will take a chance with you?" and "Where does one start?" It has been done and is being done. Everyone who has sold a manuscript had to start somewhere and you can, too.

One of the things a publisher considers a definite plus is an attractive, articulate author who is willing to go the PR circuit, appearing at book signings, talk shows, lectures, seminars, civic events, and mall openings and has a record of publication in periodicals and newspapers. It also helps to be a recognizable member of that elite group of movie stars, retired generals, aspiring politicians, popular columnists, serial killers, and talk show hosts. For the majority of working authors this route is not a viable alternative.

Of the very many books published in any typical year, on average, less than two hundred of them are first novels. The path to fame and fortune is sometimes cleared through the good graces of a graduate school professor. The dream of every student is to be offered a six figure advance directly from academia. It doesn't happen frequently, but when it does, the lucky author turns out to be the best student in the post graduate class of a highly respected professor in a first rate college. If you find such a jewell and he agrees to be your mentor, he may even make the all important phone call to an editor he knows personally.

If none of the above classifications are available to you, don't despair. The chance to find a new literary voice is an opportunity hard for any industry professional to pass up. For those of us who are past our school days, attending a writers' conference is a good opportunity to bring your work to the attention of a qualified mentor. If you can convince the seminar leader that you are sincerely interested in pursuing a career as a writer, you might be fortunate enough to bring your skills directly to the attentive ear of someone influential who is working in the industry. The character of the writer, his willingness to follow his individual star, his love and enthusiasm for his work, all count favorably toward his chances of success. The early years of successful authors reveal they will have pursued a reasonable period of training accompained by the determination to endure some sort of apprenticeship. It is self evident, that every published author was the first person to believe unquestionably in his own ability. By far, the majority of manuscripts find their way into print fueled solely by the single-minded determination of their creators. It is that "stick-to-it-tiveness" that provides the capacity, that, in the absence of recognition, motivates one to improve to the point of mastery and the resulting respectable sales.

WHAT IT TAKES

The many characteristics that go into the making of a best selling book are as numerous as the authors. One universal characteristic of the majority of writers is the love of language, not necessarily manifest in flowery verbs and adjectives, but an ability to write clearly and concisely, to look generously at the human condition, to hear speech and to reproduce colorful dialogue. Whether the pleasure found in reading develops early in life, or, at last, in the sunset days pondering life's meaning, the respect for books and book makers is a natural outgrowth of that passion. One day, in a most unobtrusive manner, the casual preference transforms into a very natural aspiration to see one's own words in print. It has always been true that writers read and readers write.

There are great variations in the education of a "(wo)man of letters". Certainly voracious reading contributes to a measure of skill in communication. Formal training in academia is another suitable background for the professional writer. Becoming an authority in almost any field lends itself to literary expression. There is no lack of paths to a career as an author.

ATTRIBUTES FOR TRIBUTE

Bringing to the public the "why's" and "wherefore's" of some new and innovative concept that has stimulated the interest of the public is a factor that may motivate a non-fiction publisher to offer a development contract to a well-recognized authority, however, if there is more than one expert involved, publishers can then make a selection from those who qualify.

Another group of people who have little difficulty in getting their material published are those individuals with extremely high visibility. Any celebrity who has achieved some measure of distinction and along with it the notoriety afforded by having a recognizable name will be a candidate for an autobiography, though the project may require a ghost writer or a collaborator to strengthen the book proposal.

Getting published is not the same as becoming a professional. People who have achieved fame in another field seldom have the skill and talent to produce a book in the brief length of time that they are in the spotlight. They require professionals to do the job for them.

Lacking a familiar name to place on the jacket of the book to attract sales, the aggressive publisher will look for a different degree of notoriety. Sometimes, depending upon the magnitude of the event, simply being in the right place at the right time is sufficient to generate that modicum of interest from the industry to place the principal in the enviable position of obtaining representation with little or no effort. Being a principal in a highly disasterous event such as a plane crash might attract interest, but it had better be a big plane and it had better have crashed ignobly in order for a contract to be offered as a result. A near miss, while it may be quite thrilling to those surviving, doesn't sell books. Though this practice is somewhat akin to ambulance chasing, it isn't quite as reprehensible, though, frequently, members of the legal profession are involved.

Unintentional participants in public events are in the same class as are celebrities. They are not sufficiently skilled to produce a manuscript detailing the unfortunate event. The more well-known the incident, the more likely it is that highly professional authors will have rushed in to cover it. The competition then is set against the track record of high profile writers. Though skilled writers can be hired either as ghost writers or as collaborators, an expedient but unfamiliar association is not always successful. Collaboration is one arrangement that should be entered into carefully. It demands close and intense co-operation. It is not always easy to find a good match of professional and amateur. (A task in which a literary agency can be extremely helpful.)

However, deliberately setting out to become a professional writer requires more than being in the public eye or in the right place at the right time. It requires the same dedication and hard work as becoming an expert in any other occupation.

The average man in the street would never consider becoming an investment banker without adequate academic preparation and practical experience, yet, there is a generally held concept that becoming a professional writer is just a matter of sitting down and writing. Creating a salable manuscript is, naturally, a necessary component toward that end, but it is not the only important element. While it may not be obvious to the aspiring writer while he is immersed in the process of creation (and we are assuming that the manuscript is excellent), the accumulation of prior literary credits is an obvious advantage in influencing the decision of the publisher. Although the unsold writer concentrates all his attention on the gradually growing pile of finished pages, the likelihood of his cherished work ending up on the shelves of the local bookstore decidedly depends upon his acquiring a degree of professionalism.

The virtuoso writer must be talented, skilled, proficient, dedicated and reliable. Cultivating such attributes takes the willingness to work long hours at one's craft, exceptional training, steady application, and writing experience. (It doesn't hurt a career to have extreme good luck, relatives highly placed in the business, or a winning lottery ticket). Commitment, hard work and perseverance are three other valuable characteristics that will come in handy for the writer with aspirations.

THE CREATIVE WRITER

Storytelling is an art; selling is a skill. By prioritizing the process of becoming a professional writer and by taking small but incremental steps both art and skill can be developed and success can be reached. Bulldog tenacity and unshakable confidence are two qualities that enhance those chances.

When holding on to the original inspiration becomes difficult, it pays to enlist the help of fellow writers in keeping that elusive goal active.

Becoming qualified for a professional career has many of the same requirements as that of any other business. Creating a business-like atmosphere is the first step. It means setting aside a time and place to work and setting up books for time and expense reports. It means structuring a viable plan for the attainment of your objectives and paying close attention to what people in your field are doing. Networking is the solution to many of the writer's issues.

ROYALTIES AND REMAINDERS

Study those authors who are at the top of their profession whose works command six figure advances and royalties of millions of dollars: such writers as Tom Clancy, Sydney Sheldon, Stephen King, Robert Ludlum, Dick Frances, Danielle Steele, and Louis L'Amour. Over the years they have garnered the rewards of mastering a popular genre: Sheldon, glitz; Steele, romance; King, horror; Clancy, action/adventure; Ludlum, international intrigue; Frances, mystery (racing); and L'Amour, western. The reason that they are able to demand huge sums of money for their manuscripts is because they have built up a following and their names alone on a book jacket are familiar to the genre reading public. Their fans are already avid readers of the genre and by doing what they do very well, they are able to command an enthusiastic and loyal readership. By staying with a particular genre, they are able to generate considerable sales for their publishers. For such writers as these, finding an agent is akin to getting a bank loan. It's easier to get when you don't really need one. Even with that advantage the best selling authors prefer having representation, leaving them free to spend their time in producing the next bestseller. A remarkable result of limiting production to one genre is the accumulation of the number of followers that grows with the publication of each additional volume.

Learning how to maintain the original inspiration is a necessary part of that achievement. Techniques for handling the problem can be found in books that writers seem to love to write about writing. Authors, especially successful ones, are always willing to share their secrets. One very good tip is not how to start, but how to keep on keeping on. Once the blush of inspiration has faded what is needed is a method for getting through that time when it seems that the muse has gone west.

The best solution for that condition is to have a clear idea of what the story is meant to say before starting. In fiction, a writer becomes stalled, not from lack of inspiration, for if that were the case, continuation would not be a problem, but from a script does not reflect the author's point of view. If it is constructed on a series of events, once the events are spelled out, there is nowhere for the story to go. If the story is not the problem, the author needs to learn improved writing technique.

Leaving off writing at a point in the manuscript where the next passage is already clearly in mind is a useful method for getting over that chasm (through which even prolific scribes have been known to drop into), writer's block. Another procedure for keeping the muses working is to write for a prolonged period without censure whatever comes to mind. Drifting and day dreaming can inspire, though it may not seem to be a part of the writing process. As Burton Roscoe said, "What no spouse of a writer can ever understand is that a writer is working when staring out of the window." With gentleness and patience, eventually, the creative force reemerges.

Behind the resolve to see a concept through to a satisfactory conclusion is the inherent belief that the spirit of creation is always nearby. Learning to tap into that energy and keep it coming is all a part of becoming prepared for a professional career. Having a vision of your objective constantly in mind and the holding on to the purpose in writing your manuscript helps to build that necessary persistence and technique.

Book publication depends on a steady influx of written material and the writer is the at the heart of that process. It starts with a visionary with aspirations mulling over what is in his mind and taking the pains to learn how to communicate, to share his internal world with those who are willing to listen. Just as the author owes his identity to his readers, the publishing world has an obligation to the writer. He is a necessary part of the industry. The need of the author for the book publisher is no greater that the publisher's need for him.

HELPING HANDS

If the prospect of sitting down at the computer in isolation for the length of time it takes to produce a salable volume is a distasteful idea for him, the would-be author can sell the rights to the story. Lawyers frequently function in this capacity. They often serve as representatives for novel or film story sales. Though they are not as familiar with the market as an agent might be, they are just as legitimate in functioning in the capacity of representative. There are favorable and unfavorable aspects to engaging a lawyer for this purpose. Lawyers are in a better position to adequately protect an author's legal rights, however, they may not know the market as well as a literary agent does and their fees, based on a different scale, will add up to more than the standard agency commission.

If the author's fame already includes a few thousand persons, all of whom are ready and willing to purchase a professionally produced manuscript, he will find the pathway to literary fame to be strewn with spending money.

For aspiring authors who have not yet achieved their full measure of fame, having a sponsor or a mentor is of proven advantage. Whether the advocate is a member of the academic community or not, access to the right industry personnel is the principal criterion. If the student is good, it is a double blessing not only for the novice, but for the supporter who first noticed and brought to the attention of the world the emerging talent of a new writer.

A favorable recommendation from an graduate instructor has the potential to attract the interest of an editor of a university publishing house. While they are not usually prepared to offer a generous six figure contract, it is a legitimate way to proceed with one's career. Being discovered by a professor in graduate school is a very common path to eventually receiving literary rewards. Publishers establish contacts with those in the academic field. Of course, you may need to raise the flag to insure the instructor notices your desire to establish a literary career.

NONE OF THE ABOVE

If, in thinking about this, you mentally checked off "none of the above", it may be wise to consider alternate means of getting published. Employing an editor or a ghost writer to go over your material with you is a short cut to producing an acceptable professional draft. If your manuscript is completed, but needs work of a more technical nature, you can hire your own literary consultant. If the problem is grammar, punctuation, syntax and format, a line editor is what you need. If you have limited writing skills, you might consider working with a collaborator.

Collaboration has many advantages, but it can be tricky for if it is to be successful, there are many elements that must be matched. Finding a partner is a very special process. Both members of the team should have complimentary working habits. The time of day when their best work is done, the special skill each brings to the alliance, their basic sense of values must be similar or at least congruous. Their viewpoints need to blend well for the intimacy of the working environment to be harmonious. They must agree on their purpose and their objectives for the work. Having found such a paragon, the task is to convince him or her to work with you.

One note about contests. Entering competitions is good practice for the writer determined to become a professional. If the contest is sufficiently prestigious, the winners are in the right place to be discovered by a literary agent or a member of the publishing industry. It is wise to keep in mind that organizations which offer awards are funded by charitable institutions which can change their areas of interest without notice. Once a competition is discovered that has possibilities, submit a request asking for the particulars and the deadlines. Enclose a self addressed stamped envelope with your request. Remember, competition is keen and it pays to stick to the rules. One other admonition. Only send your very best work. As the saying goes, "There is only one chance to make a first impression."

There is a section in the back of the Writer's Market that lists many national and regional competitions. Competing is a good way to hone skills, learn to write to specifications and to call attention to your work. No insignificant benefit is the award of the prize money which is always of interest to a self employed person.

Whichever solution you select, you will find plenty of help in every community ready to assist writers who are willing to continue to learn and improve.

Chapter Three
****

THE BUSINESS OF THE BUSINESS

"How happy the life unembarrassed by business."
- Pubilius Syrus

"The best business you can go into you will find on your father's farm or in his workshop."
- Horace Greeley
(just before he advised a Western departure.)

If the legendary rewards of six figure contracts are dancing in your mind and you are not dissuaded from pursuing a life of fame by the demands the public makes on its celebrities, then perhaps you are the one in every four hundred "wannabees" fated for outstanding literary success. If this is your dream, and you succeed, you can look forward to lionization, affluence, ease and a lifetime of following your bliss. Even if the laurel of luxury evades you, you will fare better than most. You will still have had the joys of indulging in your favorite pastime and the heady rewards obtained in pursuit of lifelong learning.

Strong motivation is needed to create any book, not the least of which is the financial reward. Though a publishing house will make an outright purchase of the work, the actual dollar amount that can be expected from any particular literary effort is unpredictable. Naturally, we all hope to be well paid for our work and visions of a bestseller keep a writer going when enthusiasm wanes. It is hard for an author to evaluate exactly what his work is worth while working toward recognition. I have heard it said that when an accounting is kept of every hour put in on writing effort, eventually, the income catches up - so keep on keeping on.

While it means a lot more book and record-keeping, it is advisable for the writer, sold or unsold, to keep accurate track of the time he spends at work. This is not only for his own benefit, but in the event he is offered an assignment and asked for an estimate, it helps him to know his pace and from that to calculate his probable production schedule from already completed material.

A system of payment that is based on a percentage of the net seems to be the most equitable solution to the compensation dilemma for both the publisher and the author. While the creator of the book may have to wait for his share, he knows that his predetermined portion of net sales is awaiting him no matter how many volumes are sold or how infrequent the payment period.

The publishing house deals with its obligation to the writer with a gradual payout over a period of time equal to the shelf life of the printing. Remainders and returns are dealt with separately. A few years ago, the tax laws referring to remainders was changed altering the forgiveness credits that publishers are permitted on unsold books. This revision, creating a new classification, makes it necessary for the publisher to be more selective in the books he buys, the books he ships and those he remainders. Once a book is returned, the publisher moves the volumes by selling bulk lots to a discount book company. Once the unsold book is taken off the primary market, whatever sales the book enjoys fall into another category.

Because actual sales records are in the hands of the publisher, it is important to be affiliated with a reputable, well-established house. If there is a problem in accounting, it is always the writer's privilege to have access to the sales records.

If a publishing house is in a strong financial condition, the company may advance a lump sum to the author who has presented an interesting proposal for an unfinished book. The advance is never in addition to the contractually established percentage, but a prepayment premium which is then deducted from future royalties. The publisher must be certain, though, that his capital investment will pay off and the author can be depended upon to complete the book as promised. The uncertainty of contracting with a first time author working against a deadline while finishing his book as promised is the reason why first time authors must present completed manuscripts while experienced writers can get advances on a proposal. Any time an advance is made, the royalties which have been contracted for are withheld until a sum equal to the advance is recovered by the publisher.

Royalties are the lifeblood of book authors. By definition, an author's royalty is the specific percentage of the wholesale price of a book as it is sold. That percentage is turned over to the author on a regular basis according to the agreed payment period once the advance has been recouped. The actual percentage for royalties is between six and fifteen percent, depending upon the experience and name recognition of the author and the contract he is able to negotiate. When a writer is part of a production team for a series, the compensation is a flat fee and there are no royalties. However, there is a great variation in the way in which the royalty is calculated, how often it is paid, whether there is to be a lump sum deduction equivalent to the advance and the terms of the payment; all make a difference between one arrangement and another. This is the area in which an agent earns her commission. A typical wording of the clause in the contract that covers the royalty payment is as follows:

> The publisher shall compile semi-annually the earnings for the work as of June 30th and December 31st of each year and will send the author a statement with any payments due, within 30 days after the end of the accounting period.

That's it. That's what we work for. Given the nature of the business, the potential for good strong sales figures is the bottom line for measuring the success of any literary effort. Marketability is the factor that determines how eagerly a writer is accepted.

Whether or not an agent will be willing to represent a particular writer depends on the potential future the agent envisions in taking on representation since agents only make their income from the commissions earned after they are able to market the output of writers under contract to the agency. Publishers are more willing to consider work that is represented by an agent, but a great many will look at unsolicited, unrepresented work.

The process of making the transition from amateur to professional begins with learning to think like a professional and by beginning to do all the things professionals do. It is a time to practice discipline; to create a special place for working; to understand the need to keep accurate records; to present and promote your work; to attend networking groups, classes and seminars; to determine exactly what your literary services are worth and to charge it; to give service to your vocation and to keep informed of what is happening in the industry.

Finding a contemporary with whom you can establish rapport can make the loneliness of writing a lot easier. Just knowing there is another person going through the same effort as you are diminishes the feeling that you are working in a vacuum. Attending association meetings helps to improve the chances of broadening career horizons. Networking not only makes the going easier, but makes the getting there more satisfying, as well.

Be willing to accept advice from others who have had experience in the business of writing, but be wary of accepting suggestions concerning your writing from friends. That task is better left to professionals. Good sound criticism can be invaluable, if you can find it. You may have to pay handsomely, but it is well worth the fee. Just having someone to guide you can make the difference between a burgeoning career and a floundering one. Enter contests. Do anything that helps you to think of yourself as a member of a select and talented group. Work on your image as a writer. A subscription to a trade magazine will provide news of writing trends and occasions to enhance your career and just getting that magazine every month will remind you that you are a working member of a profession.

Look for opportunities to add to your writing credits. Experience with publications of any kind is valuable even if it is as a contributor to a local throw away newspaper or even the editor of a high school paper. Clubs are always in the market for reporters and it is possible to get press credentials by doing community service. Little theater groups feature works-in-progress and most libraries hold regular programs of story telling. Whether the writing is for performance or for print is of no consequence. Don't overlook coffee shops and book stores which serve as excellent "farm clubs" for emerging writers who are willing to use local resources. Whatever the writing task is, if it will add to your background, accept the offer. Continue your training. Offer to read your works in progress and continue to enter competitions.

A ROSE BY ANY OTHER NAME

Using a pen name doesn't get you out of paying taxes, but under some special circumstances, it is necessary. Just keeping funds separate from family earnings is reason enough. There are several classes of writers who don't have the option of writing under their own names. Ghostwriters, of course, are always anonymous. When a sponsor hires someone to write for him, he will generally stipulate that the authorship shall be in his own name. On occasion, collaborators will use an alias to distinguish their collaborative work from that created individually. Unauthorized biographers, very frequently use a pseudonym, simply for protection of their sources. On occasion, a scorching expose may be published under a pen name.

Writers-for-hire who are working under a production contract may find that the name under which their work is being published belongs to their employer. For example, paperback publishers do this quite frequently. Male action adventure series which feature the same characters and locations throughout a succession of volumes will be published under one name belonging to the publisher. My first client held such a contract. He was unable to use his own name as author of the adventure novels he produced at the astounding rate of one every six weeks, nor was he able to take it with him when he went to another publisher. Name ownership guarantees that the series publisher will be able to contract for a specified number of novels during a limited period. Heavy volume producers put out as many as six novels a month. High quantity production situations such as this, which would be difficult for one writer to produce consistently month after month, use a common name for a stable of writers assigning unified authorship to the entire series. In the case where the publisher has had a great hand in launching the career of a writer, he will want to maintain the rights to the use of the name in the likely event the author's success catapults him to another publishing house. This name will have been copyrighted by the publisher and will only be used for a particular series.

Men use women's names and women use men's names under some conditions. Felicia Andrews, Debrah Lewis, Aurora Moore, and Victoria Gordon are among the forty or so female names used by male authors who write romance novels under women's names. Women who write murder mysteries may opt for a male sounding name, like P. D. James. The rationale is that books sell better that way. At least that's what "they" say and it would be wise to believe "them" considering the amount of marketing research that publishers of paperbacks do. In truth, some prolific writers who are attempting to break into an entirely different style of writing may use a pseudonym.

If you are writing an exposé, and the book represents a point of view that reflects badly on one's employer or an employment situation, a fictitious name might be the better part of discretion.

Authors who produce more than one style of writing find it practical to use a different name for each; a tough sounding name for a detective novel and a softer sounding name for a romance novel could conceivably belong to a single author.

Obtaining a pen name is a very easy thing to do. It is accomplished in the same manner as is a DBA (doing business as). All newspapers have available forms for that purpose which can be had for the asking. The name, then, is published in this standard form for four consecutive weeks in one selected local paper. Instructions on the exact procedure can be had from the newspaper by requesting them. The circulation isn't important so you need not seek out the newspaper with the widest readership.

Opening a bank account expressly for the purpose of creating a professional entity makes record keeping and tax accounting easier and less complicated than lumping income and expenses in with the family fortune.

RENDER UNTO CAESAR

In-home office expenses are accepted as a legitimate business expense and are deductible provided the area claimed as an office is used exclusively for that purpose and enough income is generated to cover the expense claimed. A proportionate amount is then allowed for real estate taxes, mortgage interest, casualty losses, or rent, lights, heat, insurance, repairs and maintenance. Some forms of depreciation are admissible as well.

Whether or not it is advantageous for a writer to incorporate depends upon whether there is sufficient income to warrant taking this step. While there are some tax breaks, you may find that the additional work outweighs any benefit. Under corporate structure compensation is paid to the corporation and the writer's salary and expenses are disbursed from total income. Of course, individual taxes are paid on the salary portion while business deductions are taken on the corporation.

The items that will be effected are: writing off the space used; the purchase of books and attendance at conventions, seminars and workshops; telephone charges and postage; personal expenses; legal advice and professional dues.

The bookkeeping isn't hard once you understand it. Keeping track of expenses is a worthwhile habit to cultivate whether or not the corporate status is chosen.

THE WORKING STIFF

Being a working writer has concomitant responsibilities along with its obvious rewards. Just as a citizen has an unwritten responsibility that demands he refrain from calling "fire" in a crowded room, a writer has the obligation to acknowledge derivative material. Very often an inexperienced writer will write to me asking how to protect his ideas. The theft of literary ideas is not a problem. It is absolutely true that there is nothing new under the sun, (well, almost nothing). Originality is not only possible in the context of any story, but the myths and megastories of every generation need to be constantly retold and upgraded to reflect the mores of the times. Just as the practice of portrait drawing reveals the work of each student artist to be essentially a self portrait, so the style and context of a narrative is stamped by the personality of the author. It has been my experience that the same story line given as a class assignment to twenty students will garner twenty different stories. There is as much room for differences between author interpretations as there is between individuals.

SO? WHAT'S NEW?

Plagiarism is defined as the use of another's material without attributing proper credit and is punishable by law. The direct duplication or imitation of words, phrases and sentences comprises forbidden activity. How then does one pass along information? Simple. One way is to ascribe proper credit as the law demands. Another is to ask the author's permission to quote and the third is to paraphrase in your own words with your own interpretation the data you are planning on using. A writer is obligated to uphold certain rules, most of which are defined by statute. When another person's exact words are used, the quote needs to be cited. If names of characters, locations and the exact sequences of events are used unmodified as in an already publicly distributed novel, due credit must be given, although, since creative writing is such a unique process, each case must be carefully decided on its own merits. The only party who can challenge the claim of proprietary interest is the person who actually created the material.

Authorization must also be specifically requested and obtained when personal details are used in non-fiction material. The same is true for the use of pictures, illustrations, charts and diagrams which are taken from someone else's work. The wording of a sample form letter used for this purpose is in the appendix. Of course, once factual information is published in the media or in reference books, and accessible to the public, permission is not necessary. Short passages fall under the "fair use" doctrine described elsewhere in this volume.

ON THE JOB TRAINING

The preparations for a writing career vary widely and because creative writing is a talent that can be developed, criteria for success is heavily dependent on application. Aptitude can be measured, but achievement must be attained. While training alone does not necessarily guarantee attainment, no amount of intention, perseverance or output can serve as a substitute for quality. Discipline in the form of study and consistent application is the most valuable attribute for the development of a writer's ability. The old axiom holds true: one learns to write by writing. The writer is no different from the serious athlete. Practice is the key to success in either case.

Actual training for a career as a writer starts with the mastery of language very early and the process continues as long as the student is willing to learn. Formal study, of course, is a lifetime opportunity. There are many advantages to a writing career that are not as readily available in other occupations. The materials for study are conveniently placed for anyone who wants them. The proliferation of story materials is one of the most characteristic features of our times. Films are offered everywhere, books are free at local libraries, book clubs abound, and video and audio tapes are as near as the closest vendor. Most libraries carry video editions of contemporary performances along with audio versions of classic books. Periodicals which can be had for minimal subscription fees are devoted to the development of writing skills. Seminars and correspondence schools devote curriculum to student's needs and convenience and accessibility of popular entertainment media is so omniprominent as to be characteristic of the electronic age in which we live. With the use of home computer data bases, research is not only easier than ever but it is proliferating as well.

Another advantage to writing as a profession is the accommodation of being able to work anywhere with inexpensive, extremely portable equipment. Even though contemporary writers as a group are adapting working methods to reflect the technical progress of the computer, literary volumes can still be produced with nothing but paper and pencil, if need be, and the pursuit of one's profession can be practiced wherever one happens to be.

With a modicum of flexibility, a writer can usually find a market for his skills. While every assignment may not require literary excellence, the burgeoning demand for information is so great that opportunities are far-reaching and varied. What is important is to realize that the activity of writing helps in the practice and development of writing skills. Another reason to continue writing is the absolute truth that inspiration comes to the writer as he writes.

Workshops and seminars are offered in many communities across the country. They are not only helpful in providing the means to continuing education but they serve as excellent focal points for networking endeavors as well. One interesting aspect of writing for a living is that, like any art, it is one profession that does not require certification, licensing, professional accreditation or any other form of validation by a government agency. The occupation as a writer is self-defined and the formulation of an individual learning program is as varied and unique as are those who practice the craft.

Writing a book can be a minor adjunct to the totality of a career, or it could be the culmination of a lifetime endeavor. Unless the writer is under contract, the completion of a book carries with it no built in deadline. Even under contract, time allocations vary greatly. Barbara Cartland writes a new novel every two weeks dictating her story to a cadre of secretaries. Helen Santmyer took ten years to write *"And The Ladies Of The Club"*.

There are incomparable opportunities that go with being a working writer. If this is your calling, one of its unique benefits is that there is no time in life when writing is not appropriate. Young or old, happy or sad, sophisticated or naive, it doesn't matter. It is an equal opportunity vocation. Neither age, nor sex, nor race, nor nationality is a limiting factor. Writing skills can be practiced anywhere and forever. There is no retirement age. Writing is suitable for those with highly developed imaginations and just as appropriate for those with tastes as diverse as abstract theory or precise realism. Memories, fantasies, and even alternate realities can all be pursued and expounded through the practice of creative writing. No language, subject or circumstance is taboo.

The career of a journalist takes its practitioners to all manner of interesting and exotic places; crime scenes, historic events, artistic performances, hospitals, natural disasters, court rooms and many other locations, both in the midst of current events and into the musty smelling halls of research libraries. No other career has such a wide and broad application with so many areas of specialization. Writers have had the responsibility to observe and record history and in doing so have focused on social, institutional and governmental ills occasionally providing the force behind the incentive for needed reform. Take Woodward and Bernstein, for example.

Another case of the writer-for-hire is the paperback writer. Series volumes are created through contractual agreements. For his assignment an experienced author will be given the characters, locations, and situations and from this commissioned start he will be asked to develop original combinations and time constraints using those assigned elements.

Writing for paperbacks is the easiest way to start a professional writing career. Such renown authors as Daniel Steele and Barbara Cartland began in this manner. The majority of paperback publishers issue the stipulations for their series. Based on extensive market research under rigid manufacturing control, a company will create exact specifications for popular literary genre. These pages are called tip sheets and can be had by writing and asking to find out exactly what a particular publisher will buy. Writing genre novels without first finding out what publishers are looking for is a waste of time.

One especially nice advantage that goes with being a writer is the widespread availability of one's peers. Writers' groups, academic institutions, media centers, theater groups, schools and community centers all support and promote clusters of writers where hints for finding work can be exchanged and information about markets can be discussed. Writer's associations provide a variety of role models for any type of writing.

The one element of writing as a career that has always held my interest is the ever present challenge. No matter what genre, what specific class of writing that you select, there is always that opportunity to channel your work into a more productive and more satisfying format that reflects even more of your talent.

The public looks at the writer as some special kind of person who mysteriously originates information out of whole cloth. The agent looks at the writer as his partner and source of endless material. The publisher sees the writer as a necessary element of his otherwise smoothly operating business. The long suffering spouse looks at the writer as a person who is averse to working for a living. A writer is all of those things and many more.

Chapter Four

****

HIGH RISE STORIES

"I personally think we developed language because of our deep inner need to complain."
- Jane Wagner

"It was a dark and stormy night,..."
- Edward Bulwer-Lytton, Baron

Storytelling has been around since language was invented. As soon as man began to make sounds, he told stories. Around the camp-fire, the caveman reported to other members of his clan news of the terrors beyond the cave. Primitive man developed language to express his needs and satisfactions. Vocalization became necessary to gain understanding and acquire cooperation through sharing the experience of his contact with the beasts and elements of nature. Before there was a need for record keeping, there was a need to report.

New uses and new techniques for communication are constantly created to meet the demands of society, commerce and technology. The transmission of information is crucial for us in today's world in order that we may deal effectively with our fellow man. We must articulate our needs and conditions so that it is possible for us to work together. This need is universal. Language, both oral and written, is just as essential in less developed civilizations as in our high tech community. We just have a more complex world in which to move about and have a wider selection of tools with which to communicate our ideas.. The electronic superhighway is soon to be a reality. Communication skills will be in greater demand as the principal tools used by our contemporary society which depends heavily on interdisciplinary, interpersonal and inter-national communication. We use language for a whole range of uses: broadcasting news, recording history, keeping up to date with current events, maintaining the law, organizing work, entertainment, making purchases, studying and many, as yet, unnamed functions. Through the eons of time, things haven't changed all that much. We still need language to report dangers to the members of our tribe.

GROWING UP LITERATE

As children, we listen to learn, to be entertained and to be validated. The most delightful and memorable part of childhood is the bedtime story. Our dearest memories are of hearing about our favorite characters and their exploits and of anecdotes about delightful animals with human characteristics. When we begin to have unique experiences while growing up, experiences which are an essential part of becoming an individual, written language provides us with the basic knowledge of what is expected of us and what our world is like. When we report our fears to the responsible adults in our lives, they are interpreted for us into lessons about our environment. Becoming an adult requires that many personal decisions be made for the very first time. The uncertainty involved in this activity creates a natural need for validation and approval that translates into a preference among adolescents for rap-type activity. There is undoubtedly basic satisfaction found in communicating personal adventures to one's peers.

This phenomena probably accounts for the tremendous popularity of films and television with young adults as they mature into full-fledged members of the community.

Value upon value is added to our common intelligence as we learn. In this way, we amass tested elemental truths. From telling and retelling of circumstances and outcomes, a pool of knowledge is developed from which rules of social conduct are eventually formulated and refined. If our experiences are good and the stories we hear are accurate, we are fortunate and the information is well received. We learn what others expect of us and how we are to behave. As we begin to sharpen our narrative skills we, in turn, contribute to the knowledge of those around us and to those who come after. In this way, our lives are enriched through greater understanding of the human condition. The best stories do this. In the popular media in the 90's, the extremes of behavior are emphasized in film, in magazines, in newspapers and on television.

CLASSIC FORM

Each creative form has its own unique conventions. Just as a sonata has a format that defines it as such, so do the many forms of storytelling. There are rules for the creation of works of art though they have common origins. The fact that screenplays are a popular art form does not detract from their highly classic nature. They are defined by their structure, length, content and design. Works of Shakespeare, unique in language construction and content, originally were created as popular pastimes for the riffraff. The Chinese woodcut was first designed to decorate the paper used to wrap export china. French courtly dances were a large part of "pop culture" of the time. The first cartoons were designed as political flyers for the public expressly for those who could not read.

Particular art forms are recognizable by their specific prototype and may be defined as "classical" although they may not have been thought so at the time of their highest popularity. While there are certain similarities in all styles of storytelling; novels, plays, folklore, fairy tales, vignettes, operas, etc., they are still distinguishable one from the other by their particular form. All are based on the dictates of storytelling and are created according to specific rules. Novels, while they may deal more with the internal landscape, still have a beginning, middle and end and, as simple as that sounds, if the author chooses not to observe that convention, his manuscript will suffer immediate rejection from the agent, the editor, the literary consultant or the publisher to whom he applies.

It is a good practice to learn the uses of the craft. While novels have a broader range than most other literary forms, they still must focus upon a main character and the circumstances of his life, even if that main character turns out to be inanimate. Traditionally, creative fiction features a hero (or heroine), a sought-after goal and barriers to its attainment. Novels are designed to be enjoyed in solitude, enhanced by the reader's imagination.

Plays for the legitimate stage, while sometimes enlarged in theme and limited in scope, are constructed following the rule of unity. Stage plays have factors in common with novels and screenplays. Musical comedy shares some characteristics of dramatic performance material and so does opera, and though, in both cases emphasis is on music, the content is that of human emotion. All performance art have recognizable elements of traditional forms. This is easily demonstrated when a book is converted into a motion picture. Almost always, something vital is lost in the translation and the movie is apt to be a disappointment unless radically altered from the original format.

I could mention theme and premise, plot conflict and confrontation, peripety, character development, story line, and crisis. There are many elements of dramatic writing, but it is beyond the scope of this book to trace the rules and patterns of creative fiction. I cannot stress enough, however, that it is of vital significance that the author understand that the application of the appropriate rules which must be recognized and adhered to whichever form his writing takes.

WRITE THE RIGHT THING

If you are a writer with aspirations of being published, the very best way of accomplishing that end is to write for paperback publication. There are more than a dozen publishers addressing this market. They have, on average, six imprints under which they release as many as a eight volumes a month. Forty percent of all books published are romance novels. Detective, mystery, horror, sci-fi, fantasy, young adult, and action adventure make up the rest. All have faithful fans. Some publishers issue five or six a month, every month. Readers of male action adventure, for example, purchase them as regularly as magazines. The low-priced paperbacks are an excellent training ground for new authors. It isn't necessary to have a recognizable name to write for this market. The high profile name on the cover is apt to be owned by the publishing house, anyway. The high volume of novels needed to meet the demand assures the new writer of a reading. It is not necessary to have an agent represent you for this market.

CONTENT AND CONTEXT

Good writing in any medium incorporates the expression of feelings and the many colorful differences in the ways that people perceive and respond, a carryover from the tales of the cavemen. Some of the other elements that make for traditional narration are: tension between characters, their conflict with others, within themselves and with the forces of nature, a tradition that began with earliest communication around the campfire.

Everyone believes he has a story to tell. In my practice, I am constantly surprised by the numbers and varieties of fledgling writers who aspire to have their manuscripts published and/or performed. The confidence and enthusiasm of first-timers convinced that they have authored that special book that will soar to the top of the bestseller lists is truly impressive and inspiring.

Each man's story is unique. Whether the telling of it may contain idyllic anecdotes of tranquil pastoral scenes or intriguing little-known facts surrounding historical events, there is a germ of originality in the story of each life. To tell that story is certainly validating and though the execution is all but irresistible, few biographies ever make it into print if the author's name is not recognizable or the subject's life is not well known. If some other content is featured with the biography used as illustration, it has a better chance of reaching the public.

If you intend to write a biography of a living person,

determine at the onset whether it will require authorization. If the public figure you have chosen to commemorate is the subject of a good deal of press, you may not need permission to use public information, but you will have to declare your book an unauthorized version. However, authorized biographies can be substantiated by interviews, pictures, documents, etc. The flip side of that is that highly public people are generally candidates for well-known, highly creditable authorship and there is little opportunity for untried writers.

DON'T CALL US - WE'LL CALL YOU

Being involved in an historic event is another author's incentive for the creation of a book, but its successful publication depends on the person writing it and his degree of involvement. If the author is a newsworthy personality, or one who has participated in some newsworthy event, the agent may find him. If you are that person and literary effort is not your forte, you may want to sell the rights to your story. Seek out an entertainment lawyer or a professional ghost writer for this particular task. Make certain that your agreement spells out the function of each party involved and be especially focused on the permissions and approvals section of the contract. It helps with publication to be the recognizably authoritative person at the center of the event. Publishers work on the theory that if the witness to a notable event will draw book buyers into the stores, the principal protagonist will attract even more.

If the principals at a publishing house have reason to believe that a contemporary newsworthy incident will produce a high volume of sales, they will likely engage a salaried writer to cover it. These writers-for-hire can be drawn from the lists of experienced journalists or free-lance authors with sterling reputations. For this task, it is essential that the person hired be comfortable with deadlines and editorial demands.

The content of the writer-for-hire paperback is subject to the needs of the publisher though for this type of commission an author might be given the character or characters, locations, and situations to use in his story.

FACT VS FICTION

The work of inexperienced writers will often suffer needless rejection when the lines between fiction and fact are not clear. If the plot line is selected from a newspaper account of an actual event or series of events, the story created to present it is apt to be colorless and dispassionate. The reason is that newspaper reports are meant to be as factual as possible, and as objective as possible, whereas the value in fiction is its emotional content. Even when writing articles focused on accounts of people's affairs, the accomplished journalist manages to be objective and detached. A creative fiction writer needs to keep in mind that event-driven narratives tend to get chronologically oriented and disconnected from the emphasis on the human values which may be inherent in the material. Stories centered on action tend to underemphasize emotional content and when they do, they disregard the process necessary for reader identification. It is much easier for the reader to recognize a universal emotion than to vicariously participate in a unique adventure and, what's more, the telling takes a particular skill. When the author persists in describing one occurrence after another without turning his attention to its effect on the characters involved, he is neglecting one half of his story.

Another cause for the publisher to reject a manuscript is the depiction of a flawless main character as the center of the piece. The literary professional knows that readers will tolerate a character as vicious and antisocial as a serial killer, if the story is interesting and the pace is good, but no novel can support perfection, not even in children's literature. The pleasure obtained from reading requires that a degree of identification be developed between the character and the reader. While the reader may recognize the human qualities he holds in common with the fictional character, no reader can identify with the perfect person. The suspension of disbelief needed for identification is stretched and the reader quickly becomes bored, impatient and disinterested.

CATEGORY FICTION vs MAINSTREAM

The path to publication taken by many best selling authors is through the creation of category fiction. Stories easily classified as to type are called genre novels. This label is placed on includes westerns, gothics, suspense, romance, sci-fi, young adult, true crime, fantasy, horror, erotica, mystery, etc.,. Mastery of any of these classifications is the quickest method for getting original work accepted. Even without the immediate satisfaction of gaining recognition and representation, in the process of developing competence skills will accrue that can be applied to all manner of writing.

Mainstream novels are composites and do not readily fall into any one category. Frequently, they will contain elements of several genres. It is most helpful to know exactly what it is you have to sell. A mainstream novel might sell thousands and thousands of volumes. Because they are published in paperback format, genre manuscripts are more inexpensive to produce and even more likely to be well received by a readership just as numerous. This is an additional reason to attempt category fiction in the beginning of a writing career. Becoming aware of these distinctions is part of becoming a professional. It helps to learn as much about all manner of manuscripts as you possibly can. The knowledge not only improves the chances of your getting attention from those who are in a position to help you, but you owe it to yourself to know your craft.

Because there are so many more opportunities for the novice writing popular fiction, competition is not as demanding and that advantage also applies to the job of getting on the roster of a competent agent as a category writer. Fees and royalties are not as high as for mainstream novels, but the ratio of paperbacks to hard covers is so great as to make it advisable for the aspiring author to consider fiction. Developing the sophistication that accrues in the writing will not only save time in getting your work put on the book shelves, but it will give you a clear idea of the market and improve the chances for finding representation.

Good children's literature is a specialized field that is always popular with agents. There is a sub-group of mythology and folklore for both adults and children.

Another non-fiction group that always has a market is the cookbook. Ethnic cooking is especially popular right now. It follows the trend toward multi-cultural works. The author coming up with an original way of presenting food preparation will likely attract an offer from a publishing company which will not only purchase the concept, but also come up with some fantastic promotion to augment its distribution. A definite plus is that you may not have to go through the process of finding an agent.

NEW WHINE FROM OLD VASSALS

Aside from the time-honored categories, there are others that, under special circumstances, call into play a new genre. An innovative class of literature that evolved within the last generation is the non-fiction novel as exemplified by Truman Capote's *In Cold Blood*, a fictionalized account based on a factual story. Television has elevated it to an art form in the very successful programming of the movie of the week features. Gore Vidal's works, *Burr, Washington, D.C., Lincoln, Empire, 1776,* and *Hollywood* are classed as "historicized" fiction, original work that has a factual background. All by way of stating that new forms can still be created.

The wants of the reading public change as the interests of society changes. The techno-thriller is currently "in"; novels such as Tom Clancy's *"The Hunt for Red October"* are enjoying wide popularity. Horror stories by Stephen King are high on the list of currently fashionable reading matter. Louis L'Amour is the reigning master of the western. Danielle Steele and Sidney Sheldon have captured the "glitz", high-ticket romance market.

The demand for feminist literature has spawned a vigorous new category as well as that of minority and gay and lesbian literature. The ethnic mixes in our cities in the nineties has produced a flourishing interest in multi-cultural material. Other rapidly growing classifications are: self-help, military history, languages and geography, religious literature, which is always in demand, and some new types of romance novels featuring older and/or even divorced main characters. Sales of detective, sci-fi and fantasy novels satisfy the hunger that people have for escape. Surprisingly, there is a more serious counterpart in the resurgent interest in essays. Manuscripts with academic tie-ins have their own smaller, more specialized but reliable and enduring markets.

Titles of popular fiction, while they cater to a constant readership always demanding fresh reading matter, do not spawn the desire for ownership that a non-fiction book does. However, lending libraries purchase large numbers of volumes for their members. Softcovers have their fans, but hard covers have their owners. Like any sales effort, book sales are a numbers game. Because the readership for a non-fiction book crosses many demographic lines, the demand will produce sales in consistent predictable numbers. It is the most prodigious market of all.

BETTING ON THE NUMBERS

To calculate the potential for your manuscript consider the classification into which your book belongs. Identify whether the fiction is genre or mainstream and whether the material is timely. Styles in the media go in and out of fashion. For example, the western film had been out of style for a full generation prior to *Dances with Wolves*. And then, it was quickly followed by *The Unforgiven*. Male action adventure is in the midst of a wave of popularity but romance, mystery and detective stories have all maintained a constant and regular demand.

If your project is an original non- fiction property, the offer for representation will be influenced by certain parameters. One such delimiter is whether the material makes a definite contribution to the body of knowledge extant. If so, it is worthwhile to take into consideration whether you have adequate writing skills to articulate the story. If not, are you amenable to finding a collaborator or a ghost writer? Are you presenting a new and distinctive point of view that will appeal to the public? Do you have a well prepared concept in a readable style? Is the timing right for your project? Are you speaking with sufficient authority?

If this is your first bid for professional status you may want to improve your chances by first making contributions to periodicals. It is a distinct advantage for authors of any type of literary effort who are seeking representation to be published in less auspicious publications first. It is prudent, if assignments are not available to you, to submit to literary magazines or small publications for little or no pay just for the benefit of getting the credit and the experience. Short stories and poetry are two classes of writing that are likely candidates for this kind of exposure. Since minor works are rarely agented, and there is no one to tell the writer that being published in any form is a big plus in the search for representation, a humongous catch 22 is created. Being unaware of this process, a writer may ignore the opportunity to his detriment. Because it is not financially advantageous for an agent to offer to represent short stories, the author may not have access to valuable professional advice that would be beneficial in this instance. Regional magazines are always looking for new talent for their editions. Getting published in a small literary magazine is a sage career move. For performance works, publication in play anthologies is also a valuable stratagem. Poetry, because the pay is so little, is not practical for a agent to take on and therefore it is almost never agented. Small literary magazines frequently offer prizes, the awarding of which is a plus in favor of the poet. Lyricists are best served by teaming up with a musician to get their songs played.

Highly specialized forms of writing are most generally

assigned to a writer-for-hire. This occurs when the rights to the work are owned by another and a free-lance writer is sought for production. Such literary works are: paperback series, the letters of celebrated people, novelizations of films, and ghost-written autobiographies. Acquisition of these specialized stories is a costly endeavor that has inherent lucrative value. Writers for television series, however, do require agents as do film writers. The Writer's Guild of America prohibits the unagented writer free and unhindered practice of his craft. I find this custom to be unique and unconscionable.

Plays and performance materials are so individual that each one must be taken on its own merits. Undoubtedly, performance material is always better if it can be presented on stage. Little theater groups are always open to mounting an original presentation as a showcase for aspiring actors. A performance is not only a good way to get exposure for the play, but evaluating audience reaction is extremely helpful in the process of rewriting. There is a market for all types of original material. Quality of the writing is not the only determinant of success, however. Professional writing is the product of a professional. Though that sounds like the description of an impossible situation for a novice writer to accept and deal with, new authors are coming up all the time, but it takes more than a talented agent to establish a career.

WINNOWING THE CHAFF

In my experience as a literary agent, It is not unusual to have casual acquaintances tell me of some idea they are certain will produce a fine story. When I tell them that ideas are not a marketable commodity, the next thing they ask me for is to find someone who will be willing to ghost write it for a lion's share of the profits. I have to tell them that, (1) I don't know of anyone competent as a writer who is lacking ideas of his own and, (2) even if I did know such a person, he would hardly work for the promise of a portion of a future disbursement no matter how generous.

Writing personal experiences are acceptable provided you are a celebrity and your story is of potential interest to the public. Fiction has a much broader license and can have any subject the author chooses. Nor is it necessary for literary works to be based on an original concept. Many a success has been created from a new treatment of a familiar premise. While there are just so many ways in which human beings can relate, there are unlimited ways to handle variations on any theme. What is of principal importance for professional acceptance of original material is the structure and interpretation.

The pattern for most contemporary fiction falls into one three types. It is either a story of a victory, a human revelation or a slice of life. The third type is better reserved for children's stories, television sitcoms, poems and short stories. Longer works need to have a bona fide hero or heroine who faces his/her own short-comings to vanquish his fears and false dreams. A drama needs a theme, a believable premise and a resolution that somehow impacts the hero.

FINDING YOUR VOICE

Writing about what intrigues, surprises or annoys you will fuel and energize your projects and give you the motivation to see it through. Abandoning the thought of the audience and the situations that impress them and concentrating on the ideas that are important to you as an author and a member of contemporary society is the way you find your themes. What is it that excites you? What is it that puzzles or astonishes you? When you have selected those concepts that stimulate emotions in you, you have found a theme. Next, determine the point of view that contains the most drama. What remains is to establish the voice that best expresses what you have to say.

It will be advantageous for the author to determine where his best talents lie. If he has a flair for crisp, concise writing, he will be more successful with a journalistic style. If his language is flowery and heavily descriptive, he will be out of place in a fast-paced action adventure. The most compelling writing is created when the author finds something he wants to say and discovers a voice to say it with.

The literary agent looks at the nature of the dialogue to examine whether it is natural and unaffected. The amount of dialogue must be in balance when compared with descriptive passages. Another matter to be aware of is whether the character is speaking with a measure of authenticity. Does he accurately reflect his time and place? What is the content of his speech? Is he relating knowledge he already has or that the audience already knows? Telling the reader what to think about the characters deadens the prose and limits the reader's participation.

Even if it were possible for an author to examine his material objectively, there are capable editors who will do it for him. It is a mistake to ask friends to do this task. Friends have their own priorities and might conceivably be more interested in remaining friends than being honestly critical should they find something in the writing that is not as good as it could be. The amateur you have invited to read your book is not capable of giving you what you ask for. It is more of an advantage to have someone with broader experience or more highly developed skills read the manuscript. Always accept the services of a professional reader if you can secure one with adequate qualifications.

Of course, different types of writing require different parameters. When you classify what you have written you will know better what you have to do to get it published. Is it mainstream, non-fiction or genre?

Don't dismiss genre material as being insignificant or less than worthy of serious effort. The writing can be just as demanding as mainstream, the market is more reliable and the opportunity is just as rewarding. By far, the majority of original writing sold is for the paperback market. Of that total, forty six percent of all paperbacks sold are romance novels and a surprising percentage of them are sold overseas. Hungary, for instance, sells 17,000 romance novels a day!

The guidelines for genre writing are quite specific. The paperback romance novel must be lively, imaginative, original and creatively written. The characters must conform to the specifications of that particular imprint. It must focus on love and devotion. The stories are plot driven and character driven. While they are formulaic to an extent, the story must be centered on the relationship between the man and the woman. They must be fantasy oriented with a happy ending. Once those parameters are met, there are no restrictions.

The counterpart of the romance novel, male action adventure has just as large a following.

Paperback publishers use vast quantities of original novels each month. Some imprints publish as many as forty or fifty novels a year. The odds of one getting published are certainly better than they are with a mainstream novel. Besides, there are hidden benefits. Even if a writer is unable to crack the considerable technique to his skills. The requirements laid down for pulp fiction are exacting but they are easy to duplicate.

What is the genre? Is it being fulfilled? Publishing houses will offer tip sheets telling specifically what they are looking for. Take seriously what you learn from the tip sheet. Categorizing your manuscript and matching the targeted agency to your submission is the best means of getting started.

The subject of the manuscript will give you the first clue. Mainstream fiction exceeds the demands of genre material. Characterization, background, time span, and scope are deeper and broader than genre fiction. If your output is in category fiction like; mystery, sci-fi, romance, horror, western, glitz or the path to publication is more clearly defined.

Non-fiction has different requirements. Is your material original and authentic? Is it factual? Do you have the proper documentation and authorization necessary for validation? Will you need releases? Are you the appropriate person to present this material? Does it qualify as professional? Does your work have broad general appeal? Is your story fictionalized? Are you aware of the difference between chronological dramatization and storytelling? Is the manuscript one of the more exotic forms, i.e., the non-fiction novel? What is the definition of a work of fiction? Does your book fill the definition? Are all the elements present? Is it timely and interesting?

What is the very best thing you can do to improve your chances for publication? The agent will welcome you as a client if: (1) you have evidenced by publication that you are already on the route to professional; (2) that you have a track record with a periodical; (3) that you have acquired journalistic experience; (4) or that you have a group of people who already know of your writing; (5) and/or you have a well-established, talented collaborator; (6) you are the creator of prize winning material. Lacking any of the above, persistence, skill and confidence will be doubly important as you send your manuscript to market.

Chapter Five

****

THE MARKETPLACE AND THE MANUSCRIPT

> "To market, to market to buy a fat pig. Home again, home again, jiggety jig."
>
> - Nursery rhyme

You've taken the courses, attended the seminars, and with the help of some great teachers and guides, you have suffered through the editing process and several rewrites. If the work you have written is non-fiction, in addition, you will have done extensive research, conducted numerous interviews and collected authentic documents. Convinced you have created a project worthy of publication, you finally pronounce your manuscript finished. Now ready to be sent out, it is no longer the personal document that you have been so intimately involved with. The pages are full, the hard work is over and you can no longer keep it to yourself. The days of keeping it to yourself are ended. No matter how dynamic, timely or engrossing an author's work is, unless the material reaches the public, it may just as well remain on the level of a personal exercise.

There is a world of difference between the amateur writer and the professional. An amateur writes solely for his own pleasure. He is required to meet no deadlines, demonstrate no assigned point of view, satisfy no content stipulations, extol no thesis, nor produce a definite number of words on demand. While he has no rigid parameters to fulfill, these factors alone do not necessarily distinguish his work from that of the professional. However, the fact that he is answerable only to himself *does* differentiate him from the selling writer. The public demands certain specific criteria in reading material. Publishers, if they are to stay in business, must reflect those tastes.

Meeting the uncompromising needs of the marketplace is sometimes a hindrance to getting into print. A professional author is a writer who gets paid for his work. He is paid by the publisher who produces reading material in a form in which it is accessible and attractive to the reader and is worthy of carrying the company imprint in the market-place. For that happy circumstance to occur, many intermediate steps are necessary. The task of putting the book into the hands of the reader who is interested in buying it and, coincidentally creating sales for the publishing house, is a highly specialized function.

A LOOK AT THE READER

Each type of book has its own audience and must be considered as a separate market. Even though the agent endorses and promotes, the editor okays, the publisher produces the manuscript and the bookseller offers the book for sale, it is the reader who ultimately measures the success of the marketing effort. The person who is a sci-fi fan is not likely to purchase books on collecting china cups. The typical mystery reader cannot be counted upon to purchase a book on ballet. The self-help reader does not buy books about military history and it is improbable that the reader studying French will want to own a collection of Ukranian fairy tales. The demographics of classes of bibliophiles are well-researched and their expected responses are carefully calculated. Sales figures are evaluated in terms of market share.

If your book is designed to appeal to a hobbyist, for example, the advertising has to be displayed where that reader is likely to see it. The same technique is appropriate for any publication. If a book is to be a financial success, it will have to be placed where it comes to the attention of that very special purchaser who will want to have it for his own.

Specialized books have secondary markets. Travel and language books sell at airport shops; carpenter's manuals sell at builder's supply stores and computer language books sell at computer stores. A secondary market for a book on diet control will sell just as well in a health food store or a health club as in a book store, as will a book on collecting toy soldiers find a respectable market in a hobby shop.

Contrary to common belief, though eventual readership defines a market, the demographics do not emerge until after publication when the actual sales figures are revealed. Quite simply, the publisher who stays in business selling books develops distribution outlets and methods of servicing them through highly sophisticated techniques of market research. The same data that is used to extrapolate and identify prospective markets is applied to the prospects for book production.

The publisher purchases the manuscript, designs not only the format but the graphics, selects the paper and prepares the advertising campaign on the basis of this data. Once the book is printed and prepared for distribution, it is then ready for promotion. Review copies will need to be distributed. If it is the kind of publication that supports ancillary items such as mugs, calendars and diverse novelties, he must secure the licensing of them. All this must be accomplished before he can realize any return on his investment. Small wonder publishers are conservative and reluctant to take risks.

Special interests, timely information, cultural trends and tastes, and technological advances all are taken into consideration when purchasing decisions are made. Publishing a book involves a good deal of risk, but by studying the demographics and needs of the reading public, book producers are able to narrow that gamble to within reasonable limits. The industry is not infallible. Every book store has a remainders table filled with overprints of books that did not sell as well as expected. That feedback from the bookstore is taken into consideration when the selections are made for the following year. By using current book sales as a guide, the books for the next list become the hope for a new, more profitable season.

This background information is valuable in helping to make for a successful publishing venture by the novice author. The agent can be of great assistance, saving time and energy. Manuscripts do not sell themselves. A strategy must be developed. The task is to find the most likely publisher who has a track record of success with your particular category. You can save yourself much time, energy and avoidable distress if you are aware of the machinations of the book publishing industry. *Knowing to which classification your manuscript belongs is essential.* Each manuscript attracts a specialized set of professionals having a proprietary interest in that particular category. These are the people who are prepared to guide the work to its eventual reader.

The market is defined as a group of purchasers who have certain specific interests in common. The more specialized the group, the easier it is to find and identify. Folklore of the Ancient Mayans is more specialized than World Myths, and while there may be fewer readers whose interest is focused on the Indians of Central America, the scholars of Mayan Folklore are more likely to want to own such a book. Curiously enough, potential sales can be inversely proportionate to the scope of the topic. You can appreciate the enormous effort required to produce a bestselling novel, since a separate readership must be created for every one.

WHAT HAVE YOU GOT TO SELL?

If the book is to be successful in finding its appropriate market, the initial step is to identify exactly what it is you have to sell. Manuscripts come in many shapes and formats. There are textbooks, story books, history books, biographies, cookbooks, children's books, romances, mysteries and books about current events and famous people, humor books, cartoon books and even books to be completed by the reader, but no matter how broad the topic or how contemporary the subject matter, each addresses its very own, very particular readership.

The importance of the market in a successful publishing venture cannot be over emphasized. One of the prime reasons unsold authors do not achieve the representation they seek or the sale they believe to be available is because they create a manuscript without considering the market. A full color coffee table book on the children's game of jacks is a worthy achievement, but a poor financial risk because of the comparatively limited number of readers that will want to purchase the volume. That bottom-line evaluation applies to fiction as well as nonfiction. The style, the language and the point of view are all elements that shape a document, but it is the eventual destination that shapes the method of distribution and ascertains its place on the shelf of the book store.

When you classify what it is you have written you will know better where to look for a publisher. Decide whether your book is right for a hard back, a paperback, a scholarly text, a trade book or for performance. Examine your material by looking at it through the eyes of those professionals who do the marketing.

If your manuscript is a genre novel, have you fulfilled its requirements? Publishers who produce genre material have very stringent requirements they offer in the form of tip sheets which can be had for the asking. The tip sheets will describe the qualities, occupations, age and life style of the hero and the heroine, the limitations of the story, the length of the manuscript and the time period which it covers.

Knowing what it is you have to sell holds the clue to all the other particulars that will lead you to an appropriate agent or publisher. It is in having this understanding of your manuscript that determines the success you have in getting your manuscript published.

Content counts for more than literary value in placing non-fiction, although clarity is important. Every author, no matter how limited or extensive his experience, will automatically write up to his highest ability. A common endorsement regarding his work is likely to be, "It's as good as anything else out there." Or, "It's a great story", or he my even say, "But my book is unique." Undeniably, it is, but there are techniques and strategies to learn about marketing that will influence whether or not his book will find the editor, agent or publisher who will invest the talent, time and energy needed to get the work to the marketplace. Every author whose work has found publication has looked into the realities of the market and taken the pains to educate himself.

FICTION

Fiction falls into several specific classifications. Novels that have the merit to generate wide general interest, enjoy large advertising budgets and substantial publication runs will be well received. Gross sales of more than sixty thousand volumes are needed in order for a book to become a bestseller. A publisher needs to see this kind of potential popularity to justify the necessary expenditure. Genre material is the most plentiful. As a class, they produce sales equal to that of mainstream volumes. However, advertising budgets are much smaller. Genre novels are available only for limited periods of time and therefore do not warrant large budgets. Romance paperbacks and their equivalent, male action adventure, are responsible for forty percent of all book sales. With detective, horror, fantasy and sci-fi classes they comprise the bulk of all book sales.

The bid for publication rights for your work of fiction is dependent upon certain precise criteria. There are fashions in fiction just as in anything else. For example: The western novel has been out of fashion for a full generation. Authors like Zane Gray and Jack London are classic authors whose sales are perennial. A resurgence in interest in the category is sparked by one or two contemporary authors, such as Elmore Leonard and Tony Hillerman, who can always be counted on for steady sales.

Detective stories are always in style. Occasionally there will be a new genre created. When Truman Capote wrote *"In Cold Blood"*, a non-fiction novel, which sounds like a contradiction in terms, he originated a new class of fiction. Its publication led the way to the invention of the true crime category. Another new classification is that of the fictionalized biography, spawning the spate of posthumously published Marilyn Monroe "biographies". Anne Rice created a fresh new demand for vampire stories and there are a spate of companies developing imprints for the contemporary young adult. Despite the enormous popularity of the horror story as told by Stephen King, the undisputed best sellers of the eighties and nineties are the techno-thrillers such as, *"The Hunt for Red October"*, *"2001"*, and in film, the Alien series and the Terminator series which derive directly from the fantasy genre.

Because of the sheer numbers of volumes sold, genre novels are not only the most readily accepted for publication, but their authors find the transition to hard back mainstream to be an easy progression. Taking into account all these factors, romance novel is still the leader of all book sales. Taken together with male action adventure, the detective story, Sci-fi and horror genres, they comprise the majority of book sales everywhere in the world.

NON-FICTION

The criteria for non-fiction are more difficult to meet than that of the profusion of fiction genres. There is a definite check list. The first thing that the professionals in the book publishing industry will question about an original non-fiction property is its authenticity. Does the subject hold enough interest for the public to provide a sizable market? If the answer is "yes", the publishers will want to know, first of all, whether you are a legitimate spokesperson on the subject. Are you a specialist in the field? The authority you evidence is a measure of your status among your peers. What is your track record? Have you already had material published in periodicals or in trade publications? That's important. If the answer to all these questions is affirmative, you can be considered a suitable proponent. That's not the be-all and end-all. Once it is agreed that you are recognizable as a specialist who has a mastery of the subject, the quality of message is the next consideration that must be determined. Do you have writing skills? If not, will you need a ghost writer or a collaborator? If so, all things being equal, that's a problem easily solved. There are professional writers who are capable of shaping your document into a marketable form, though they will demand compensation for their services. You may be able to employ a writer who is interested in the project and whose reputation is well known.

That isn't the last requirement that you will have to satisfy, however. Given an acceptable plan and a surrogate that you can work with, the next element to be examined is the content. What is it you want to say? Does it contain a fresh and distinctive point of view? Does what you have to say make a valuable contribution? And finally, do you have a well prepared concept in a readable style? If all of these points have been adequately handled, your chances of getting into print are considerably improved.

Many manuscripts I have received compare well with those of highly paid writers, but if the subject of the work is one that has received attention in the media, the commission to write the book may have already been assigned to an published author already under a contract arrangement.

While selecting the market is best done before starting the manuscript (a substantial factor in the careers of best selling authors like Isaac Asimov, Barbara Cartland, Raymond Chandler, Agatha Christie, Sidney Sheldon, Dick Frances, Stephen King, et al), it is doubly significant after the fact. Is your material original and authentic? Is it factual? Are you the appropriate person to present this material? Does it qualify as professional? Do you have the proper documentation and authorization necessary for validation?

Depending upon the nature of the personal information included in your work, you may find you need to have a release. If so, simply send a certified copy of the portion of the manuscript that pertains to your subject asking for permission to print. The subject of a story will be interested in its accuracy, but more than accuracy is needed to interest a publisher. Of course, if your story is fiction or a roman à clef, no such authorization is necessary.

When writing from a life story, take special care to see that your structure is more than a verifiable laundry list/chronology. Be certain that you have more than a collection of place descriptions and a selection of dialogue enriched scenes to offer. It takes more than the dramatization of a series of events to produce a marketable manuscript.

Truman Capote, in his breakthrough novel created a unique genre form that is widely copied. While his style is overtly cinematic and his structural methods comprise several styles of writing, his novel gave respectability to the concept of creating a work of fiction overlaying a true story.

I have repeatedly made reference to genre as a standard. If you follow the practice of creating novels according to tip sheet specifications, your work will automatically conform to the needs of the publisher and your acceptance will be more likely. Once you have established a track record, you can create whatever form you wish, just as Truman Capote did for true crime fiction.

Regardless of the originality demonstrated by the writing, there are established factors that determine its acceptance. Novelty is not the criteria for publication. Ideas are everywhere and frequently crop up from several directions at once. Under these circumstances, the author with greater authority will be most successful.

Narratives of personal experiences lacking a substantial built-in market - "pre-sold" is the industry term - are limited in their appeal. Sales are difficult if not impossible without a huge, intensive advertising campaign. The publishing company is concerned with the potential for ROI (another business term; this one means return on investment). The publisher is going to look for a book that already has an intrinsic readership. Chances of attracting publication are much better if one is a celebrity, and even more so for one with a large following. Take note. Elvis books are still on the shelves years after his death.

It is not necessary for your book to be a totally original concept. An original treatment of a familiar idea is perfectly suitable. The truth is, most material is derivative. It is the writing style and/or point of view expressed that makes the work exceptional.

Writing about a sequence of events rather than about the human condition is one tack that many inexperienced writers use. If an attempt to classify it as fiction, regardless of the dramatization, it is invariably rejected. More about this in the final chapter.

If you are not a professional writer, you may decide to sell your rights to someone who is capable of telling your story. In this case, you have several more options. You might consider an outright sale. Here, a lawyer can represent your interests and oversee the legality of the contract. In this way you will be adequately protected. While having a lawyer in your corner may guarantee your legal rights, do not expect the lawyer to know the market as well as an agent does. If you have qualms about the protection afforded you, you can always have the contract examined. The best candidate for representation is a literary agent or an entertainment lawyer, one who is a specialist in this particular sort of transaction.

WHO'S ON FIRST?

What about first novels? What are the chances of one being picked up by a publisher? First novelists who have secured five and six figure contracts, all have come highly recommended, either by a writer already under contact to the house with good strong sales, the sworn endorsement of a graduate school professor who exalts the undiscovered talent of his favorite student. It also helps if you are one of the small group of people who are highly visible, who are willing to hustle, who are comfortable making public appearances, amenable to promotional tours and book signings, sitting in on radio interviews and TV talk shows. It also helps to photograph well. About one hundred and fifty first novels were purchased by major houses last year; one hundred and fifty out of the thousands of manuscripts competing to be one of the sixty thousand books that were, in fact, published. That figures out to be one in four hundred of those that were actually scheduled for production and we have already pointed out what a long shot that is. All this discussion about probability is not designed to discourage you from your efforts. Quite the opposite is true. It's the agent's job to worry. That's what he is there for. If there is a message here, it is for the author to persevere. Taste in writing has a subjective element. The hard facts about publishing only prove that good material is hard to find, so don't be discouraged! First novels do get published and it can happen to you!

Remember, bestseller lists are created by the publishers through their awesome power of distribution and advertising. The art of creation is only half of the equation. The science of selling is the other half. Keep thinking about those one hundred and fifty first novels that made it last year. Just as every journey starts with a single step, each bestseller starts with a first page.

Whether the work is fiction or non-fiction, it must have many of the same elements. It must make use of drama, tension, suspense and discovery. There must be a logical and satisfying ending to the story which must follow the conventions of the times in which it is presented. Taking all these things into account, the first requirement is for the book to be attractive to the reader.

In controlled demographic studies, the publisher and book store owner keep track of factors that influence the buying reader. They measure the sales potential of any prospective volume with scientific precision and care, as though their future depended upon it - for it does.

After having established the existence of a potential market, finding a volume to fill that need is explored. Other elements need to be considered. In evaluating the feasibility for the publication of a non-fiction book, the same factors apply as do those for fiction. Is this the writer's first bid for professional status? Is there an established readership? What is the writer's track record? The publisher will want to know whether he is familiar with professional procedures, can meet deadlines and can work diligently under stress of editorial demands. Is the material original and authentic? Is it factually correct? Is the author the appropriate person to present this material? Does it qualify as professional? Is there proper and sufficient documentation? What about the authorization necessary for authentication? Will releases be necessary? Does the work have broad general appeal?

Having a track record of publication is a definite plus when it comes time to submit. There are several ways to qualify as an experienced author. Entering writing contests is an excellent way to bring your work to the attention of a publisher. Writing with a well established collaborator helps. If the author is an authority, articles of his based on the subject will substantiate his professionalism. Excerpts or chapters of the book published in periodicals will act as confirmation of broad public interest.

Likewise, it makes good sense for a teacher or seminar leader, who has moderate sales with a workbook, to court a wider readership through the publication of class material.

No matter how dynamic, engrossing or timely an author's work is, it cannot be considered a success if the task stops when the pages are full. The hard work is over, but unless the material reaches the public, it may just as well have been created for personal satisfaction alone.

Admittedly, facing the task of getting a manuscript into print means that time must be taken away from the process of writing. A whole new procedure must be learned and mastered, but it is not as difficult as the work involved in creating a book and far more satisfying, for it is the printed book that tells the world who you are and what you do.

Mounting a campaign to get your work into print is the most worthwhile pursuit that a writer can engage in. For the author, it is an opportunity to become more than he already is. Not that the actual task of producing a book length manuscript is in any way less if it is not ever published. The act of printing does not affect the quality of the writing or the overshadow the enormity of the job. But it does show the caliber of the creator in a way that no other achievement does and it brings public attention to the interests and the capability of its originator.

There is a world of difference between amateur and professional. A professional is one who gets paid for his work and helping to reach that objective is the job of the literary agent, the literary consultant, the editor, the publisher, the publicist and the book seller. All these knowledgeable people are waiting for the writer to put in motion the raw materials of book publication. It is at this point that the writer looks for an expert who has experience in handling creative material, who knows the market, and who is there to show him how to proceed.

Chapter Six

****

THE COPYRIGHT

The law is a sort of hocus-pocus science.
- Charles Macklin

Few rich men own their own property. Their property owns them.
- Robert Ingersoll

And nothing we can call our own but death.
- Shakespeare King Richard

Where the routine is rigorously proscribed by law, the law and not the man must have the credit of the conduct.
- William Hickling Prescott

Ownership of intellectual property is a right defined by United States law. It has changed over the years and promises to change even more in the near future. The most recent change occurred on January 1, 1978 which modified the then existing Copyright Act of 1909. As we approach the widespread use of the information superhighway and the availability of data, the legal use of an author's original work will need to be appropriately controlled and credited. In the process, many questions must be answered. Many new regulations will be developed for protection and control of intellectual property. New laws will be based on precedents set by contemporary copyright statutes.

Naturally, work that is developed for purely personal use is exempt. It is only when work is published does the law apply.

The A work is defined as published by the Copyright Act by " the distribution of copies or phono-records of a work to the public by sale or other transfer of ownership, or by rental, lease, or lending. The offering to distribute copies or phono-records to a group of persons for purposes of further distribution, public performance or public display, constitutes publication. A public performance or display of a work does not of itself constitute publication."

For the purpose of maintaining control over proprietary interests, the government of the United States has set up guidelines in the body of law defined by copyright. The rights to intellectual property are protected in the same manner as the rights to real estate. They can be rented, (optioned), leased or sold, or even subject to division. All rights apply. In most cases, like real estate, they cannot be used, altered or modified without express permission of the owner.

The specific law covering registration of creative property is Title 17, U.S. code. It refers to all manner of original materials; literary, dramatic, musical, artistic and certain other intellectual works. The work need not be published in order to be afforded this guardianship.

Section 106 of the Copyright Act grants exclusive rights to the owner of original works that enable him to control all print presentations, including reprints and copies. Distribution of the copies also is protected. Sales can only accrue to the recorded owner. All modifications, revisions and alterations, such as, dramatization, translation, musical arrangement, recording, filming or choreographic productions are prohibited without specific permission. This applies to all public performances.

When these clearly defined rights are abridged, it is a violation of U.S. law and punishable as such. With a few exceptions, the holder of copyright can apply to the federal courts to obtain redress.

There are some limitations to the law, however. The most notable comes under the concept of "fair use". All material, quotes, excerpts, abridgements even though protected by copyright may be used for review purposes, for newspaper, periodical and television criticism, for classroom study, or for brief summary comments, in limited amounts that have no effect on the market, no permission is needed. The segment must be only a sample of the total for it to qualify for exemption. Sections 107 through 118 of the Copyright Act state that the purpose to which the sample is put will be the determining factor. The words, "Compulsory license", spell out the need for compensation due the holder of the copyright for specified royalties and for compliance with statutory conditions under the Act.

While the creator of the work is the one legally granted the copyright, the means to protection are not accorded to the author, but to the particular work. Each individual opus must be separately registered and separately dealt with.

If the work was created while the artist was under hire, the copyright belongs to his employer. When he leaves the employment of his mentor, he may have to meet certain requirements to obtain copyright privileges for himself, if he is indeed granted ownership. In this case, agreement must be obtained from the employer who is the holder of the copyright under law.

Certain classes of citizens such as children, felons, the incapacitated, or individuals otherwise disenfranchised by state law may be subject to local business restrictions denying the right to copyright registration and pursuit of protection. In these cases surrogate owners can apply and may be appointed trustees.

There are fourteen classes of copyright and each requires its own document. Every form of creative endeavor falls into its own particular class. They are as follows: Books (Class A); Periodicals (Class B); Lectures or similar productions prepared for oral delivery, (Class C); Dramatic or dramatico-musical composition (Class D); Musical composition (Class E); Maps (Class F); Works of art, or models or designs of works of art (Class G); Reproductions of works of art (Class H); Drawings or sculptural works of a scientific or technical character (Class I); Photographs (Class J); Prints, pictorial illustrations, and commercial prints or labels (Class K); Motion Pictures and photoplays (Class L); Motion pictures other than photoplays (Class M); and Sound recordings (Class N).

If you would like to order your application by phone, you can do so by calling any time of day or night. The number of the Copyright Office Hotline is (202) 707-9100.

Counter to what most people believe, there are things that cannot be granted copyright registration. The law specifically excludes items such as: titles, names, short phrases, and slogans; familiar symbols or designs, lettering, variations of typographic ornamentation, or coloring; and the listing of ingredients or contents. Ideas, procedures, methods, systems, processes, principles, discoveries, or devices, as distinguished from a description, explanation or illustration are also denied copyright.

Universal concepts in general use do not have specific ownership, such as: calendars, height/weight charts, tape measures and rulers, schedules of sporting events, time- tables, lists and tables taken from public documents.

Items designed for recording information also do not require copyright. Undeveloped forms such as: time cards, account books, diaries, bank checks, score cards, address books, report forms, blank charts and diagrams, etc., are also. Forms designed for subsequent use have blanket exemption.

Inexperienced writers who offer ideas for development are surprised to hear that they are not eligible for protection. Ideas, according to the law of the United States, are in the air and despite the proprietary attention given them by their authors are everybody's and anybody's property.

Once a concept is developed, it is a different matter. Manuscripts developed in private and uncirculated can be copyright protected. Work need not be published, sold or made available to the public in order to enjoy this privilege, provided copyright ownership is indicated on the work as prescribed. When an unpublished manuscript does not contain notice of copyright it falls into the category of public domain and becomes public property. By omitting the notice, all rights of ownership will be denied. An author who circulates an unmarked volume will lose all rights and once the work is published the opportunity for ownership is lost. For any of several reasons, since it is so easy to do, it's a good idea to claim copyright for all completed works. It is easy to neglect this one detail in the heat and enthusiasm of sending out a few copies to friends, agents or publishers but it is a serious mistake that can be easily avoided.

Unquestionably, an original work privately held may not be appropriated by anyone under any conditions without the authorization of the author, formally registered or not. There are two ways in which any manuscript may qualify for registration. Prepublication registration by the author is as binding as registration in the Office of Copyright. The first, by the author, is called Common Law Property and is regulated by state law.

The benefits of copyright for unpublished works are automatic and are good until the work is published or statutory copyright is obtained. All that is needed is for the author to declare his copyright and comply with the same conditions as for published works.

If this option is chosen, however, another registration may be needed after publication. All copies of the work must be marked by copyright notice.

Statutory copyright is that protection afforded by the federal law but within certain parameters. The privileges of statutory copy-right registration are granted prior to publication for the following: musical compositions, dramas, works of art, drawings and sculptural works of a scientific or technical character, photographs, motion pictures, and works prepared for oral delivery. Software, too, is protected through copyright, though the methods to be used for the information superhighway are not yet codified.

The notice, itself, has two parts. The first is the name of the copyright owner (or owners). The second is the year the work is made public. This is ordinarily the year in which copies are first placed on sale, sold or publicly distributed by the copyright owner or under his authority. If copyright protection is claimed prior to registration, the earlier year is used. The form of the copyright looks like this:

© John Doe   1994

If the author chooses to request an official record of registration for an unpublished work, the following three items are required by the Copyright Office. The first is (1) an application form expressly intended for the appropriate class into which the work belongs as indicated above; (2) a complete, clearly reproduced, authentic non-returnable copy of the manuscript along with (3) the required fee for unpublished works of $20.00. Fees sent to the Copyright Office in Washington should always be submitted in the form of a money order, check, or bank draft made out to the Register of Copyright, never in cash. Also, just a note here that is apt to be overlooked, especially since the packet consists of several parts. The registration is less likely to be held up and more liable to receive prompt attention if all necessary parts of the submission are mailed in one parcel. Secure all documents in a sturdy parcel. The address to which all three required parts must be sent is:

THE REGISTER OF COPYRIGHTS,
LIBRARY OF CONGRESS,
WASHINGTON, D.C. 20559

The notification of copyright protection is described in the law to be displayed in a very special way. Either the word "COPYRIGHT", or the abbreviation "COPR." is sufficient. It is preferable, however, to use the symbol © which is recognized by members of the Universal Copyright Convention. Since the exact time of statutory copyright is not known, it is advisable to mark all copies with the official symbol whenever any copies leave the author's control.

Once copyright is established or granted, or is in the process of being granted, notice needs to be affixed to all copies of the book produced thereafter. The placement of the symbol and date need to be put in the proper location on the title page or the obverse of the title page. Any additional data placed on the same page with the notice.

All copyrights granted in the United States follow this exact conformation. Without adhering to this specific arrangement, the copyright is not considered genuine.

HOW LONG DOES COPYRIGHT LAST?

The official date of completion is the date used to determine the start date for reckoning the length of time the work remains in exclusive ownership. Twenty-eight years is the length of the first term of statutory copyright. Beginning on the date the work is published indicated by the notice of copyright, or, in the case of unpublished works the date it is registered in the Copyright Office, ownership is officially acknowledged as having been created on the date of registration. Sometime during the last year of the original term of copyright measured from the exact date on which the original began, an additional period of protection may be established for a second term. The copyright ends on midnight of December 31st in the last year of the copyright. Under the law of 1976, the renewal is granted for a period of forty-seven years, making a total of seventy-five years total. The renewal process is similar to the original application. The request for extension can be made to the same office using Form RE along with the registration fee appropriate at that time.

INTERNATIONAL COPYRIGHT PROTECTION

One need not be a native or even a citizen of this country to be afforded a copyright in the United States. Depending upon the country of he author's citizenship, special conditions may apply. Protection is not automatically universal. Not all countries recognize United States copyright.

The specific treaty governing international use of materials created in the United States and covered by US copyright is called the Berne Convention. The Title of the pamphlet is International Copyright Relations of the United States, Circular 38a and can be obtained from the Copyright Office, Library of Congress, Washington, D.C., 20559. The quickest way of finding out whether a specific country is a party to this treaty is to inquire of a patent attorney who may be able to give you the needed information.

TRANSFER OF ASSIGNMENT OR STATUTORY COPYRIGHT

When a book is sold to a publisher, a new record of ownership necessary. The author's name is still shown on the copyright page, even though the publisher has acquired the right to print and distribute. The transfer can be accomplished by official transfer or assignation. The sale must be in document form in writing endorsed by the original owner of the rights. The entitlement is submitted to the Copyright Office and duly recorded. Once that happens the document can be returned. Ninety days is the usual period of grace between official ownership. If the sale is to a party offshore (overseas), six months is allowed.

The rights to any work are contingent upon following these requirement precisely and will be permanently lost unless all published copies bear a notice of copyright in the form and position described above. Once distribution occurs, it serves no purpose to add the notice to copies of the work, and, furthermore, doing so may be illegal. Remember, the process of registration only establishes the exclusive right to reproduce, publish, distribute, produce or market the matter and form of a literary work. That right can be challenged and originality can be questioned. Should this matter be contested, ownership, and thus royalties, must be left to the courts to determine.

COPYRIGHT PROCEDURE FOR PUBLISHED WORKS

When an eligible work is sold, there are a few things that must be done to maintain rights of ownership. The steps taken for an unpublished work apply including a precise record of any revisions or additions to the original. Two copies of the published work with the copyright notice in place printed with the date of completion of the unpublished manuscript as well as the year of its publication are the data required for transfer purposes. The claim for copyright with the appropriate form of application should be sent to the Copyright Office promptly to transfer ownership.

When a publisher buys a manuscript it is his task to prepare the new documents and to register the transfer. An entirely new copyright is created to reflect the change of ownership. All permissions needed prior to transfer must have been obtained so that ownership is unencumbered.

There are some situations in which violations of ownership rights must be properly established and such matters as plagiarism must be remanded to a court of law. These infractions are difficult to ascertain, offenses hard to prove and penalties hard to collect. It is much more prudent to settle ownership disputes amicably before they deplete everyone's (but the lawyer's) resources. In addition, legal action is a distraction and an inconvenience to a working writer. The best use of one's time is in performing the most rewarding occupation, a good axiom to follow, especially for writers.

SECONDARY MARKETS

The same rights of ownership apply to subsidiary rights markets, that is, works translated to another form. All literary rights, which include any material which may be owned, or to which the author has, in legalese parlance, any right, title, share, interest, or control, including, but not limited to literary, dramatic, and musical material, books, plays, dramas, stories, recordings, motion picture, radio and/ or television programs, formats, outlines and any other classifications and permutations you can possibly think of are all intellectual properties and as such fall under the umbrella of the original registration.

INTERNATIONAL STANDARD BOOK NUMBER

To distinguish each volume that is produced anywhere in the world there is a system of a world wide identification numbers which has been in use since the late sixties. There is a different ISBN number for each edition and each binding of every book. Using the number avoids errors in identifying the books ordered, shipped, received, invoiced, archived, etc., A typical ISBN number might be 0-9626331-1-9. Here, the initial "0" indicates a book originating in an English speaking country. The "9626331-1-9" identifies the publisher. The suffix "1" indicates this particular title and edition of the book, hardcover or softcover. The last number, "9", is a check digit which is a mathematical function to make certain the rest of the numbers are correct, that they haven't been miscopied or transposed.

The ISBN is printed on the copyright page of the book and on the right foot of the back cover or jacket in 12 pt. OCR-A type. OCR-A is the universal typeface which is readable by optical scanner readers. Anyone may apply for an ISBN number. This useful designation is not issued by the government but by a private company that records and publishes this number. The company can be reached by mail, by phone or by fax. To receive the pamphlet detailing requirements for being granted a number and an application, you can obtain the documents by writing to the Reed Reference Publishers at:

>International Standard Book Numbering Agency
>R. R. Bowker Company
>121 Chanlon Rd
>New Providence NJ 07974

To reach the R. R. Bowker Company, call:

>Phone: 1 - (908) 665 6770
>Or: 1 - (800) 521 8110
>FAX: 1 - (908) 665 2895

The title of the material you will need to request is the "Title Output Information Request Form" and a "User's Manual". There is no charge for this information. The cost for having a block of numbers assigned to you, depending on the size of your publishing facility, is $115 and the process takes about fifteen days.

LIBRARY OF CONGRESS CARD CATALOG NUMBER

One additional registration which may be needed for books in general distribution is the Library of Congress card catalogue number. The LCC number enables subscribers to the Library of Congress' catalogue card service to order books by number and thus eliminate the searching fee. This simplifies the ordering process. Some retail stores require this number for tracking sales.

LCC numbers appear on the copyright page of each book along with the copyright designation. They are used to identify the volume in lists and reviews appearing in the leading journals of the book trade. The Library of Congress Card Number differs from the from the ISBN in that one ISBN is assigned to each edition of a work (hardcover, softcover, etc.,). The card number is assigned to the work itself, regardless of how many editions are printed or bound. This number is essential if you plan to sell to libraries or schools. The National Union Catalogue in which the listing is published is subscribed to by most libraries around the county and is issued four or five times each year. The address for this information is:

>CIP Office,
>Library of Congress,
>Washington, D.C. 20540

The title of the document containing the information you will need to obtain an LCC number is: "Procedures for Securing Preassigned Library of Catalogue Card Numbers" and their "Request for Preassignment of LCC Number" application (form 607-7). The number when obtained can be used for inclusion in the copyright application, if desired, but it is not necessary for obtaining a copyright for the work.

CLAIMING YOUR RIGHTS

Rights of ownership, if they must be settled in a court of law, become very expensive and proof is difficult to establish. Notable cases, such as that of Art Buchwald and the Eddie Murphy picture "Coming to America", prove that the author sometimes wins, but the process of bringing suit takes "deep pockets", and the one who prevails may have to wait a long time for a resolution. It is much better to be careful with the derivative material that is used than to risk a prolonged, uncertain legal battle. These problems are better solved by the parties involved without resorting to legal processes.

Chapter Seven

SQUARE IN THE MIDDLE

> "Of all of the things you cannot do - most of them are because you haven't ever tried!"
> — G. Stern

> "By nature of the business, every writer is an entrepreneur."
> — Mindy Bingham

The crucial step for a writer in becoming a professional is getting his book published. Preparing the completed manuscript for printing, distribution and sale is the goal. There are several ways to do this. Using a literary agent is only one way. Faced with the option of whether to be represented by an agency or to represent one's self is a decision each author must make according to the availability of a willing publisher, the amount of work the author is prepared to do and the time available for his involvement. Before undertaking the responsibility, some additional work is required that may take some research but direction and guidance in this area are readily available. The process is not complicated or difficult. With a minimum of guidance and a maximum of confidence in the work, it can become an interesting and thoroughly satisfying task. Having created the manuscript, the author is an expert regarding some very significant elements. He will know who the expected readership will be and even be aware of their book buying habits.

IS THIS MOTHER A NECESSITY?

Not all creative writing demands that in order to be sold one must be professionally represented. In some cases it is appropriate for the writer to deal directly with the publisher. Most paperback or genre-publishers will accept unsolicited, unagented manuscripts. If you write to the publisher asking for the company tip sheets you can find out whether they require that your work be offered by a literary agent or not. Check in Writer's Market to see if the publisher you have selected will read your novel without an agent's recommendation. If none is necessary, then you may find it more expedient to handle the submissions yourself.

If that is your circumstance, you still have a choice to make. While some publishers do not demand that you be represented, having an agent is still an alternative. The decision is one that will effect the direction you take with your work. First of all, there are factors that you need to know to determine if you should handle the submissions yourself. How can you tell if using a literary agent is for you? There are several issues to explore that will help to answer the question.

After evaluating your manuscript and carefully determining its classification, compare it with the descriptions in Writer's Market or Literary Market Place. You will find the names and addresses of publishers who will look at your manuscript without benefit of an agency's recommendation. With minimum guidance, it may be perfectly acceptable for you to do the work of getting the book published by yourself. The process is not difficult and everything you need to know is outlined below. Keep good records and be persistent in your efforts. A manuscript is seldom, if ever, accepted by the first publisher to see it. Persistence is the key.

I GAVE AT THE OFFICE

The format for submissions to a publishing house is slightly different from that of submitting to an agent. A publisher will not perform any consultation functions as will an agent, so be sure that the manuscript is free of grammatical and syntax errors; that it is in the proper format and that you have included all the information that the publisher needs. In addition to the material submitted to an agent, the publisher will want a formal proposal naming the other books covering the same subject currently in book stores. Check to see if you have followed the model for the fiction/non-fiction organization in the chapter on submissions. If you have not been published before, he will want the entire book.

Begin by having a proof read submission ready. If you are to perform the same functions as an agent, it is prudent to look at just what is entailed in representation. The job has several different aspects. It is the agent's first responsibility to evaluate the book in terms of the current market which you can for yourself by visiting a book store or checking out the book section of a reputable newspaper. You will need to understand the demands of the publisher. He will want to know whether other like publications have met with success. He will expect the contributor to be aware of the current market. If editing or revisions will give the book a competitive edge, he will expect that it will already have been done.

Knowing which publishing house is the most likely candidate for a sale is the most important thing to learn. If you see to it that the submission is in first rate professional format before sending it out, the publisher will welcome your manuscript. Make the necessary phone calls and keep records of submissions. Practice clearly and objectively describing the work to industry people in terms they understand. Just don't bother to tell him that all your friends liked reading it. That has no bearing on his evaluation and will only mark you as sentimental and unsophisticated.

There are some technical things that an agent does that may not be familiar to you, most of which you will not need to know until after being presented with an offer. The majority relate to contract negotiations, a concern you can put on hold until later.

Book contracts vary a good deal but with a little perseverance they can be deciphered. Which clauses can be compromised and which cannot are matters that the agent would end up asking you about in any case. Just keep accurate records of correspondence and make notations of all phone calls including the date and subject discussed. If the book is a smashing success, you will have the satisfaction of having done yourself a favor.

From the list of chores that an agent does, a cursory evaluation seems to indicate that most of it can be done by the author. Though for some it is of great benefit to have an agent, especially when it comes to payment schedules, but if things really get complicated at that stage, it is always possible to have someone negotiate terms. Admittedly, it is preferable to have a professional doing the necessary tasks the first time, but there are contrary reasons too. The most obvious consideration is the fee that every agent gets for his services. The ten percent that an agent is paid is equivalent to an eleven percent raise. Is it worth it to you to undertake the task yourself? What is the precise value of the agent's job to you personally? Are you willing to take the time away from writing? Is the time spent representing yourself as well spent as it would be working on your next project? How much time are you willing to put in finding an agent. What are the advantages and disadvantages?

SIX OF ONE AND A HALF DOZEN OF ANOTHER

Finding an agent can be a long process, requiring special data, skills and contacts. It can take as long to find an agent as to find a publisher. Rather than spend the time, energy and money in the service of getting an agent, perhaps it is more prudent to spend that time looking for a publisher if in your particular situation you need not really have professional representation.

Representing yourself is not impossible and there are some factors in its favor. There are probably people around you who can help. Do you have access to a network of writers who have been through the process, who can answer your questions and bolster your morale? You may be the one writer in ten who can get to a publisher directly. Access to an open door is a huge plus that may outweigh all the other considerations of whether to seek professional representation or go it on your own.

The crucial issue of whether or not to undertake this task is a personal one. First, and most apparent, is the question of whether or not you are willing to do the job. The actual work of representation is not for everyone. Whomever undertakes the project will need to investigate a few things about the various publishers who are as individual and distinct as colleges are. To make the connection with the right one who is looking for your project is not complicated. The information you need is public knowledge easily located in the library or book store.

Part of being a professional is knowing what's being sold. Librarians need to know that, too. The way they stay current is to subscribe to a magazine called Publisher's Weekly which offers subscriptions to the public. It contains extensive lists of books being offered along with reviews of contents. The listing contains the name of the publishing house issuing the volume.

Book stores reveal a wealth of information. Just looking at the amount of space a genre is allocated tells you about the tastes of the book customers in that area. Another source of valuable information are the store's clerks. They work in book stores because they love books and you'll undoubtedly find them willing to discuss publication and sales with you. I have found book store clerks to be well informed and always interested in talking to their customers. Introduce yourself and tell them what you are doing and don't be shy about asking for their input.

TWENTY QUESTIONS - TEN ANSWERS

Deciding to represent yourself means that you must learn the answers to some very pointed questions. False starts in attempts to find the publishing house that handles your type of material can be embarrassing, not to mention the myriad of rejections that having an agent will field for you. That is probably the most difficult part. If you just remember that you only need one publisher, the procedure will be easier to endure. Tales of multiple rejection notices received by established authors are legion; two dozen are not unusual.

To make the commitment means being totally honest with yourself. Answering a few questions will help you to decide. The first one is a very big one: Can you be objective about your work? If you have a problem with that -- and why shouldn't you? -- you have accomplished what you set out to do. You have written a novel - but self representation may not be comfortable for you. Unbridled enthusiasm got you this far -- (and there is no question that you are better off not having to face the unexplained, off-handed dismissals characteristic of the industry) but now clearheadedness and objectivity are essential.

Be conscientious when you ask yourself whether you can be objective about your work. It is essential that you present yourself and your work to publishers appropriately in a detached and professional manner. That first impression is the only one there is the opportunity for. In the submission process, you will be dealing with editors whose job it is to dispassionately evaluate your project. You will have researched other books in that field. Being well read helps with this part of the process. Wherever you send it, they'll want to know your evaluation of its selling potential including that of the competitive books already published. You wouldn't have created the book without some reading background so capitalize on it. If the publisher was an authority on the subject, he wouldn't need your evaluation.

If you do your own work, you will need to have the discipline to keep accurate records. Simply collect the names and addresses of all the venues with possibilities and keep track of them. Sending the manuscript to the same publisher twice is as costly and useless as skipping a publisher who is likely to be interested.

As your own agent you will have to research publishers and contact them personally. You will have to know what to say to them and you may be put in the position of having to answer questions about your work. (That's one thing an agent can do while he provides a buffer from the hard realities of the publishing industry.)

Ask yourself if you will have the unflagging determination to send out your work time after time. Don't forget, no one knows your work better than you. Do you have the emotional strength to continue to cherish the manuscript that has come back wrinkled and torn? Or with pages missing? Are you faithful to your vision? Would you have the heart to print over the frontispiece and retype the cover letter to a new addressee taking the same joy and pride in each rewrite as you undoubtedly exhibited when you sent it off the first time? It is not difficult to see frustration rise to the surface.

Editors invariably have a clear idea of what they are looking for. Maintain a clear and steady attitude about what you have to offer.

If being your own representative intrigues you and you think you can do the work, developing an immunity from discouragement is the principal consideration. It helps to know that the success or acceptance of a manuscript submission is a numbers game. Very often rejection has little to do with the merits of the writing. Selections for publication are made on the basis of a balance in the publisher's list. For instance, if the company has just published a mainstream novel that has been very well received, the recently published manuscript may be more of a factor in the decision to accept or reject yours than the manuscript you are hoping to have accepted. The genre, too, is important. If a best selling author under contract to them is writing in the same genre as you, your project may be rejected to save them from marketplace competition. Because the reasons for rejection are frequently accompanied by a form letter with no explanation, the process can be maddeningly frustrating. Under such puzzling conditions you have to hold on to the imagination that brought the book into being, the vision of getting it published and the persistence to see it through, regardless of acceptance or rejection.

Trends in reading have a tendency to flood the publishers with a particular classification. Neo-realism, true crime and cultural history are now enjoying greater recognition than they have for a long time. Self help books have peppered the market for the last few years. Knowing what comes next is tantamount to knowing the name of the next bestseller. Economics have had a profound effect on cutting back all publication in the nineties. Publishing house consolidations, too, have had their impact. Where there used to be twenty or thirty publishing houses, there are now fifteen. A conservative attitude where risk is concerned also influences book purchases. At best, submission is always a trial and error procedure. I have never heard of a book being selected by the first publishing house approached.

Keep your goal before you of the day when you will succeed in attracting an offer to publish. You have as good a chance to be successful as the writer who is professionally represented.

Despite all the strikes against the unsold writer, he may nonetheless be successful. Every best selling author started somewhere. Even so, the obstacles to self representation do not begin to outweigh its benefits. Knowing exactly what the status of your book is at all times is a great comfort compared to the long dry periods that happen when you are simply at home waiting. Direct contact between author and publisher will give the author a realistic picture of what the industry is like, a valuable education for any writer.

STAMPING OUT THE MIDDLE MAN

There are a few drawbacks to self-representation. You will have to be willing to forego submissions to publication houses which will not accept unagented material. Chances are those publishers only buy material from known writers. Publishers make their profit on the books they sell. The search for worthwhile commercial material is conducted by well-educated, well informed, technically skilled and authoritarian editors. Their job is to select manuscripts that show the most promise. They depend upon literary agencies to do the preliminary screening for them. Smaller publishers take more risks. They care more about each book on their list and are apt to treat their writers with more consideration.

Before undertaking the job of seeking a suitable publisher directly, seriously consider what happens after having your book accepted. Prepare to sharpen the necessary skills to handle the marketing of your book. Get a start on promotion. Even with an excellent publisher you will want to be sufficiently prepared to cooperate in the marketing. You can always engage a PR person, someone who can direct and oversee the best publicity, book signings, and media coverage. You can hype the book yourself, as well.

After finishing a book, the job of finding a publisher can be a welcome change. There are vast differences between writing a book and looking for publication. Writing is solitary; self agenting is gregarious. Writing is subjective, self agenting is detached and objective. Writing is abstract, self agenting is definitive and calculating. Creativity deals with what is unique, while agenting is largely comparative. Furthermore, you will be all the more knowledgeable when you write your next book. Publication is the definitive measure of the professional. If you consider your writing to be an unalterable calling, the demands of the profession are just another part of the territory.

TO DO OR NOT TO DO

If, having educated yourself on the demands of publication and found that you do not need an agent to accomplish your objective, one day you may decide to take that big step yourself. Friends and relatives have given your manuscript their approval. Flushed with pride and determination, you make the move, imagining a huge advance and even fatter royalties. If you follow the directions for submissions in this book you are prepared to try your hand at it. It certainly is worth a try.

THE REEL THING

Hoping to see it grabbed up and in print before your next book is finished, you square up the pages and photocopy a replica of your masterwork. You try sending it out to a few publishers, but they have sent it back to you accompanied by nothing but a regulation form letter, a reproduction at that. The business of rejection is hard enough without even being accorded the courtesy of a personal response. Unfortunately, most readers and editors affiliated with publishing houses are too busy working with the authors they already have under contract to spend time evaluating unsolicited manuscripts. One or two of the publishers you sent your manuscript to wouldn't even look at it, much less give you the feedback you need so badly. Instead you get ... something about - "We are certain that your book is a fine manuscript. We will be glad to look at it when it is submitted by an agent." Well, that's better than receiving that impersonal photocopy.

There is always the possibility that you will strike pay dirt and your manuscript will be accepted. You may be offered a contract by the publisher at the outset. Things are going great! Remember, you will still have the opportunity to engage a representative agent to negotiate for you even after you receive an offer. There is nothing lost by attempting the job yourself.

Learning about your profession is never lost time. Getting to know how publishers function will help with the placement of all future writings.

A PILE DRIVER

If you are not experienced in dealing with editors and publishers, or have little interest in the business aspects such as contract negotiations, having an agent negotiate for you once you have an offer is a lot easier than it would be without one. To paraphrase an old saw: the best time to get an agent is when you don't need one. Having someone competent and knowledgeable on your team will help to guide you and your manuscript though the process of obtaining publication.

Keeping a positive outlook and holding that vision of a successful book in print is the most valuable attribute a writer can have. None of this work is wasted. Even if your book is not picked up, an editor somewhere may remember you. One of my most delightful remembrances is when an reader called me up six months after he had read my submission. He wanted to know how I made out with it. There was a valuable lesson there. (He became one of my best friends and writing buddies. No way I would let a fan get away!)

A WORKABLE CONCLUSION

If you are able to secure a contract, you will have travelled the route taken by many others and you will have had a worthwhile experience. Whichever means you take in the future, you will have gained some understanding about what it takes to get a book published. What is important is to realize that writing for a living is a profession and like any other requires guidance, study, practice and amassing of experience. Through the process you will learn what is readily accepted and what is not. Gordon Burgett tells it well, "Professionals sell, then write; while amateurs write, then try to sell."

Chapter Eight

****

THE PUBLISHER

It is not the quality of the writing so much as the aggressiveness of the publisher and the capital behind the release that makes for a successful publication.
- anon

THE BOOK STOPS HERE

There are big publishing houses and small publishing houses and they are measurably different in their ways of operating and their book needs. The largest of the publishers are Simon and Schuster, Time Publishing Group, Harcourt Brace Jovanovich (recently changed hands) and Warner Books. They all have imprints. Imprints are companies that publish under the name of the parent company and use their corporate resources like distribution, advertising, funding and selected in-house staff members. There are smaller publishing houses that turn out to be controlled by big publishing houses. For example: Dell publishing Group controls Dell Books, Dell Trade, Laurel, Laurel Leaf, and Laurel Trade. Harlequin produces Gold Eagle, Silhouette, Worldwide Library and Harlequin. Within Harlequin are many divisions: Harlequin American Romance, Harlequin Super Romance, Harlequin

Presents, Harlequin Temptation, Harlequin Romance, Harlequin Regency, Harlequin Intrigue, Harlequin Historicals, and, by now, there may be a few more. Each division has separate and distinct requirements and functions as a individual company. The same is true of Gold Eagle, another imprint under the Harlequin umbrella.

Rather than making your decision on which publishing house to send your manuscript to more complicated and confusing, this departmentalizing makes your job, and theirs, easier. The satellites each have their own lengths, plot line, hero and heroine descriptions and life styles, time periods, and degrees of sexual involvement, etc.,. The specific information about each category can be obtained by writing to the company for their tip sheets. It is mandatory that you know exactly what it is that they publish. These immense corporations have revenues in excess of billions of dollars. That is definitely big business.

The smallest of publishers may only print and distribute as little as one book. The majority, however, will release somewhere between twelve to fifty books per year. Which is right for you? That depends more upon your manuscript than the size of the publishing company. First of all, your project has to fit in with their particular needs. They have to want to publish your book. Each house, each year, creates what is called the list. It consists of management's plan for publication. The determination of exactly what the nature of this list is, is made according to their successes and failures in the previous years. Most houses, if they are not strictly limited to a certain genre, will do better with a group of titles within a particular range, say popular culture, self-help, gardening, regional material, etc. Their policy then will limit purchases to that special group.

When you have matched your subject matter with the publishing house, you will know better how to develop a marketing plan. With that requirement out of the way, the factors influencing whether you should go with a small press or large press are; in the case of the small press, greater individual attention results in a more customized marketing plan; a larger company may have a recognizable name and be better funded, but your script may pass through many hands on its way to the book store.

It is human nature for the writer to focus all of his attention on the difficult process of acquiring a publisher. Knowing exactly what and how a publishing house operates may seem like a moot point when "any port in a storm will do". The object is to have the book accepted. Whether the concept of a publishing house is viewed as a Godsend, paving the way to the answer to a writer's dreams, or some nameless, faceless enemy that stands between the writer and that elusive sign of career fulfillment, it is helpful to know as much as possible about publication and the people who make it possible.

When considering which publisher to seek for your book, the question of self-publication comes to mind. All of the things that a publisher does for a writer can be done by an individual. The design of the book, the creation of the cover, the jacket and back cover copy, selection of paper, graphics and fonts, securing the copyright, the library of congress number and ISBN number are all easily obtained. However, there are other things to consider, the most significant of which is the time and effort it will take to learn a second occupation. Always keeping in mind that this second vocation takes time away from writing, it is not difficult to acquire the knowledge to print and distribute your own book. The principal consideration is the actual selling of the book and the key to successful sales is identifying and locating your market. Lecturers, presenters of seminars and high profile people frequently have success in self-publication. If you are one of those persons, or if you have a hobby with a very well defined interest group, you will have targeted your market and know where and how to reach it. This is the best guarantee that you will be able to create sales and distribution for a self-published book.

Once having printed the book, the problem of storage must be faced. There are fulfillment houses which store, insure and ship for the self-published author. The facility will keep track of the books shipped and bill you accordingly. Having solved that situation, all that remains is to make the fulfillment facility superfluous once all the books are sold. The task remains of finding the market and reaching them. The next step is to mount an advertising campaign. Specialty newsletters and periodicals are excellent places to acquaint your prospective readership with the book. All manner of specified mailing lists which are for sale provide a source for directly reaching potential sales.

Participation at conventions and book sales events is another way to move the volumes into the hands of the reader. Periodical advertising works for some volumes. All these processes are a guarantee against having your garage a permanent location for dozens or hundreds of unsold volumes. Despite the complexity of self-publication, you may find it a worthwhile endeavor as an adjunct to building your career.

It's axiomatic to state that the publisher is in business to make money. However crass, that elementary fact is the basis for all the decisions made regarding the purchase of submitted manuscripts. Addressing an application to the appropriate house will save not only time in getting into print, but also the nagging disappointment of not knowing the basis for rejection.

Publishers vary considerably in the types of manuscripts that they select or reject. While some houses may favor mainstream material, others history, and still others biography or mystery stories, each has its particular preferences and preoccupations. It is customary to find one imprint which deals principally with mystery, one with science-fiction, one with true crime, action adventure, romance, etc. There are further classifications within any one group. For example, there are hard and cozy detective fiction categories. Science-fiction has many possibly subcategories.

Let's follow a book through the publication process. Before it is considered for purchase, a reader or editor will have read it. The first decision made concerning publication is based on whether or not it impresses him as a quality opus. Excellence, however, is not the only criterion. A book may be excellent but not meet other requirements. He will next determine whether the work fits the identity being created by the publishing program for the year, and whether they or any other publishing house have any comparable book already slated for publication. The receiving editor makes a judgment to either reject it or move the project further along in the decision making process.

He creates a report to that effect and, if all factors are favorable, offers it to the other staff members for their approval. One by one they read it as time allows. If one of the staff is not enthusiastic about its potential, the book will likely be rejected. If there is universal interest, it is then judged according to how it fits the philosophy of the company and whether the book is up to their professional standards.

The advertising department then creates a sales campaign. If the sales people consider that they can sell enough books to make publication financially worthwhile, they then consider both the track record of the author and of other similar books currently in circulation. Only when they are all satisfied that the potential for return on investment is really there, will they go ahead.

THE STAFF

The staff of every successful publisher consists in a carefully assembled team of like-minded individuals. It follows that the projects that they acquire are those which are unanimously attractive to that team of editors. Even though an intake reader may report favorably on a book, invariably, the selection must please the entire staff. In turn, the editors are prone to select material similar to that with which they have been successful. It is this winnowing process that contributes to ever greater specialization.

THE NATURE OF THE BEAST

Publishers, editors, book store owners, and reviewers are all dependent upon the response of the reading public and are guided by their choices. It is the book buyer who is responsible for the success of each book and ultimately the book publishing industry. Each publishing house, imbued with its special quality, relies on sales feedback for direction. Retail targeting is related to and fashioned by the books and material they propose to market. This factor, which in large measure must be approximated, is determined primarily by past successes. If a publisher has had a phenomenal sale he will naturally attempt to repeat that success. This fact alone accounts for the great numbers of sequential books published by relatively few writers. Publishers take their cues from the book store owners who are very much aware of what it is their customers like to read and are willing to purchase. "Nothing succeeds like success" is the operational premise here. The books are placed in the stores by the distributor, who provides the store owner with stock. He, too, is selective, choosing only those works he is certain he can merchandise. Even books which are accepted but whose sales seem questionable may be returned to the publisher within days.

Feedback is routed through the distributor who functions between the book store owner and the publisher. The success or failure of a book comes in the form of repeat sales, creating second and third printings, or, conversely, the assignment of the volume to the remainder section of the store or the discount book sales house. The volumes that do not "move" are books that eventually land on the big book sale table. Word of additional printings is the good news that miraculously turns to gold for the writer. The news regarding remainders is not ordinarily given to the author, which is just as well. Who would want to hear that kind of news?

I can remember looking over those tables filled with publishers' overruns and thinking of the disappointment of the author after having put his best effort into the creation of a salable novel only to find it selling for a few dollars on the discount table. No publisher can estimate the exact number of volumes he will be able to sell. Remainders are remainders after all and not a tragedy.

BESTSELLERS

While ultimately, it is its popularity with the reader who creates the sales which classify a bestseller, it is the publisher who formulates the process. If the work is general fiction, the sales effort is directed toward the name of the author relying on the following he has accrued. If the name of the author is not well known, the subject or the story line, if timely, will be featured in posters, media advertising, give-aways for reviews, television ads, newspaper ads and radio interviews. Advance exposure heavily financed by the publisher augmented by a high profiled author is the most promising route to big sales.

For books about current events, news-worthiness, as demonstrated in magazine and media coverage, spotlight topics likely to be selected for the development of non-fiction books. These books require speedy publication to meet the timely demand. Point of purchase displays and advertising count heavily toward impulse buying. These books need a lead time of at least six months to a year. Holidays influence not only sales, but advertising, as well. The big holidays are responsible for the greatest percentage of book sales. Christmas, of course, is the best occasion for a gift book. Coffee table books are big sellers in season. Gardening and sports books have greater sales in spring and summer. Cook books sell well all year round. Special promotional tie-ins shape the focus of sales campaigns. Presidential elections give rise to authorized and unauthorized biographies.

For books that do not fall into any of these non-fiction classes, the publisher and/or bookseller relies on a slow build of purchasers fueled by favorable book reviews, distribution of bound manuscripts, study groups, book clubs, and readings in book stores and attention from specialized social and professional groups.

The best stimulus to a new writer's success is word of mouth, (a factor which can be manipulated to a slight degree by extensive publicity), which requires steady sponsorship allowing time to work its way. Passionate commitment by the author helps to encourage those who have the responsibility for sales. Marketing demands patience and persistence on the part of all associated with the release of the publication.

Ethnic and multi-cultural materials benefit from tie-ins with civic movements and observations, but while these categories have good consistent sales, they seldom achieve bestseller status. The same is true of scientific breakthroughs chronicled in book form, although, as with most books, it takes at least one and a half years from completion before the book is ready for the public. Of course, books produced on demand can be created in a matter of weeks. The Branch Davidian disaster at Waco, Texas, spawned three books within a month of the tragedy.

Keeping in mind the need of the publishing house to get a good return on the original investment and the factors which determine the creation of bestsellers, of what benefit is this information to the author? Essentially, the more he knows about the business of publishing, the easier it is to understand how the publisher looks at the writer. The association between writer and publisher is one that must function throughout the shelf life of the book and for that reason is crucial to a favorable experience stemming from the entire publication process.

RESPONSIBILITIES AND REWARDS

What do the publishers do that warrants the lion's share of the take? Why is it that the best of writers only get royalties of six to eight percent of the retail value of the books they write? What makes publishers so all fired selective? Publishers put up their financial resources, that's true enough, but in financial arrangements in other industries, the usual split between the creator and the sales, is fifty/fifty. In publishing a ninety/ ten split is standard.

Imagine now that the hypothetical Optimum Press has purchased the book. The primary task is to assign an editor to go over the manuscript for accuracy, language, syntax and grammar. Will there be an index? A glossary, charts, illustrations? All those elements are discussed, approved and then created. Next, it is brought to the legal department to ascertain whether there are any points of the law that may be questioned with its publication. When it passes that hurdle, a graphic designer is chosen and he selects the font, the graphics and the aesthetic aspects developing the "look" of the book. The copyright is obtained, and an ISBN number assigned. The weight and color of the paper and the cover are proposed and selected. The decision is made on the binding, glue, and paper jacket.

At this point the publishing company may do a market research investigation to identify the best way to present this book to the marketplace.

The printing, color separation, and cover design are approved and copy is written for the cover back and jacket inside cover. The release will be timed to coincide with the remainder of the list and the number of the copies to be printed for the first edition will be determined. Tantalizing quotes are culled from the book's more intriguing passages and they are sent to the advertising division.

A plan for distribution is arranged and contracted for. A storage facility is secured. A fulfillment house undertakes to ship the book in proper allocation units to the retailer where it is to be sold in concert with the advertising campaign replete with radio interviews, book signings and complimentary copies shipped to reviewers.

The sales force of a large publishing company may number as many as a hundred people. A few times through the year, they will congregate to go over the list. These seasonal convocations resemble corporate conventions. The management introduces the list and the sales department is given direction for the marketing of the volumes proposed.

Once the book is in the book stores the publisher maintains the records of sales and expenses charged against the book. He carries insurance to cover the valuable merchandise. He arranges for complimentary copies to be sent to prestigious reviewers and designs advertising copy, provides for its display, purchases ad space and exhibits displays at trade shows.

With the cooperation of the author, the publisher may arrange signings, lectures, radio coverage, television talk show interviews and, the more daring may even arrange publicity events. When the publishers decide that the sales are going well, they may order a second printing. Of course, if there are not sufficient sales, the book goes to remainder sales tables and the publishing house takes a bath in unsold copies.

Any publisher, having command of all the resources needed for publication and understanding the nature of book sales would have no reason to hesitate hiring an experienced writer to produce a manuscript on demand.

If someone at the publishing house has reason to believe that a contemporary incident will produce a high volume of sales, they might engage their own choice of writer to cover it. These writers-for-hire can be drawn from the lists of experienced journalists or freelance authors already known to the publisher. For this task, all that is necessary is that a reliable author be comfortable with the subject, with deadlines and editorial demands. If the writer can produce, he will have found himself a wonderful way to earn a living. Of course, staff fees do not equal royalties, but then it should be worth something to have all the uncertainty taken out of the occupation.

Ex-editors and publication staff members having experience, contacts and a wealth of knowledge about the book publishing industry will gather together to form a book producers corporation. After considering marketing prospects for an idea that appears to be noteworthy, they will take it to a publishing house to negotiate a deal. If the concept is acceptable, the book producers will hire the talent to write it. They hire editors, designers, and printers for what will be the basis of a privately published book. Considering it is pre-sold and created under salary, book producers always make a profit, albeit off the backs of the hired talent. Writers are usually so overjoyed to get "a real job" that they gladly participate in the working arrangement that they have been offered.

Another example of the writer-for-hire is the paperback writer. For this assignment the writer will be given the characters, locations, situations, events and time period. He will be commissioned on a contract basis for coming up with an original manuscript using the prescribed elements.

THE ART OF THE DEAL

Publishers will generally ask for the rights of first refusal which means that, along with the original material, they will have the right to examine, evaluate for publication, and possibly bid on subsequent productions of the author whose first novel they have agreed to publish. Launching the career of an unknown writer demands a team of publicity and promotion people and funds to make the name recognizable. When the publisher takes the responsibility of taking his writer to the market, he wants to know that the effort he makes on the first manuscript is going to pay off - perhaps with the second.

Before undertaking to establish a novice writer, a publisher will have some questions that he wants answered. He will want to know whether the writer is going to be willing to help promote the book? Will he be cooperative in regard to appearing on talk shows and attending press conferences? Will he be attractive to the reading public? How about the question of first refusal? Ultimately, publishers, editors, book store owners, and reviewers are all dependent upon the response of the reading public for the success of their business. It is the men and women who buy the books who ultimately determine what will be published.

What is demanded of the author from the publisher and how is it usually couched? Typical trade books or mass-market book publishing contracts first identify the state in which the contract is made, the binding nature of the terms and the rights and obligations of each party.

Publishing agreements vary from two pages in the Stein and Day agreement to close to twenty pages in Simon and Schuster's agreement. For the writer's benefit, it helps to include a performance clause to set down expectations he holds with respect to the publisher. Items cover: the number of volumes proposed, advertising and distribution efforts conducted and requirements for second editions. These terms are not written in stone, but while they cover all points in most contracts, they do tend to favor the publisher. Get advice on the clauses that most effect you and decide what you must have, what you can do without and on what issues you are willing to compromise. Advice is available. If you do not have an agent who can interpret the contract for you, you might want to employ an entertainment lawyer who knows all about writer's rights. A caveat now is worth a lot of disappointment later on.

There are no figures kept on the loyalty of authors to publishers, but it is common industry knowledge as to which houses are the best to work with as well as which ones do not treat their authors with fairness and appropriate deference. This is information that is discovered through personal experience -- and a lesson devotedly to be learned.

Chapter Nine

****

ON THE WAY TO THE WEDDING

Hail the Bridegroom -- hail the Bride!
When the nuptial knot is tied.
- William Gilbert

Oh, let us be married, too long we have tarried.
- Edward Lear

Presenting your manuscript for acceptance is similar in some ways to introducing your bride-to-be to the prospective in-laws. The goal you are after is a working arrangement with a group of people who, until now, have been strangers, who are going to look at the new family member with cold, dispassionate eyes. Hopefully, the merger will offer both factions approval, loyalty, encouragement, and if you are lucky, better fortune than before you got together. In the process of securing an alliance with a book publisher, you are scrutinized by silent judges in a manner not unlike your evaluation by your family in a nuptial situation. In a pre-agreed arrangement, the family offers their good name and you promise to represent that name in a way that bestows honor and prosperity and is acceptable to all parties. Together you present a workable union for all the world to see.

Your initial presentation is of win or lose importance. Every aspect of the proposal must be as scrupulously gone over as is its content. Whoever said "Don't judge a book by its cover", was not said regarding the practice of literary agents and publishing house editors who consistently make critical decisions based on just such matters. This is one instance when the adage does not pertain.

To improve your chances of obtaining support for the publication of your book, you must demonstrate that you are ready for a professional career and that your material is of the highest calibre. Keep in mind that once you obtain backing, all those who undertake the task with you will be working at their own expense. It is not only your work that is on the line, it is the occupation, energy and resources of the professional who literally becomes a working partner. He will be giving of his time on the belief that all involved will prosper. In order for that happy event to transpire, the manuscript needs to be more than competitive. It needs to be distinguished by its superiority.

AN UGLY DUCKLING IS NOT A SWAN

While no book was ever published simply because the document, regardless of its merit, was presented in a readable form. Its appearance may have influenced the reader's decision-making process, either for a favorable or an unfavorable impression, all else being equal. A possible refusal is not a risk you would be wise to take, especially, since there is no need. It is immediately obvious to the recipient opening a query letter whether the request is to be taken seriously or not. The determining factor reflects back to the author and whether he has taken his petition seriously. His passion and conviction are made visible in the appearance of the presentation.

A pencilled-in, scrawled, handwritten note on yellow legal lined paper warrants a loud harrumph, no more. The hasty, ill-planned presentation is taken as evidence that the writer has not given the utmost thoughtfulness to details, and by implication will not value care and attention from others. Furthermore, the chances are slim that the careless, hurried writer will respond cooperatively to the suggestion of rewrites or welcome demands for a more precise and thoughtful effort on his part.

Neatness is of paramount significance. Submissions that are clean, erasure free, with print properly placed on the paper, without smudges, coffee spills and grease spots are an absolute necessity. Details such as taking care that the paper is of uniform quality throughout: in weight, color and content, 8 1/2" x 11", a good quality paper, (although twenty pound, white, 25% rag content is preferable, every day variety of typing paper is perfectly acceptable). Avoid the use of easily smudged paper, such as those with erasable-finish.

It is time for an appropriate warning. All these recommendations are valuable references. Though the publisher or agent will, in all probability, be receiving numerous submissions at the same time, it is not prudent to create highly original presentations. Unusual manuscript formats only serve to call attention to matters other than the quality of the work. Once the submission is in the hands of the agent or editor, it may possibly be duplicated and passed around for others to read. At this time, the one inch space provided by those carefully constructed margins can be used for editorial notations. A precisely formatted sheet is your best representation and there is much to be said for a conservative, conventional presentation.

Type should be on one side of the paper only and executed in a clearly readable font. Courier 10 or Courier 12 font is preferred. Merit is the only qualifier for acceptance and anything that distracts from the professionalism displayed in the text is more apt to be a deterrent than an aid. Computer generated hard copy is used everywhere now. Most dot matrix printers today are of such high quality that the copy is equal to that which is printed. Some publishers may ask for originals but the majority of agents will accept photocopied hard copy. Some will take PC disks, but it is prudent to inquire first. It is a good idea to inquire whether or not the editors you are dealing with will accept your format. What is absolutely essential is that you retain the original for yourself.

Text should always be double spaced and margins should be held to one inch on all edges. If your manuscript is a screenplay, it should be bound with a cover of heavier stock or plastic sheeting to protect both end pages. All other material should be presented in loose sheets. Unless your submission is meant for performance, such as a staged reading, a theatrical or a screenplay and destined eventually to be acted on the stage, the manuscript should be left unbound. In the frenzied quest for that perfect manuscript, readers and editors like to flip pages aside as they leaf through the printed words.

There should be a title page containing the name of the work which should centered and in capitals. The name of the author is placed beneath the single word "by" which is also centered. The address of the author or where he can be reached should be placed in the lower right hand corner. A phone number is not mandatory but should the reader want to ask a question, as a matter of convenience, it will save time. The use of a copyright has to do with ownership and is discussed at length in a later chapter.

Page numbering can take many forms. A single sequential system is satisfactory for most applications. If it is likely that the document will undergo revisions, at this pre-publication stage it is better to restart the numbering with each chapter.

Place the chapter number followed by a dash then the page number on the upper right hand corner of the page. A simple header need only be suitable for the purposes of identification and requires no more than the name of the author and the name of the work placed in the upper left corner.

The length should be appropriate to the form. A novella can run upwards to 30,000 words. For genre material, the exact length will be specified in the tip sheet. A mainstream novel can run more than 120,000 words, although that is a long manuscript. Be sure to note the word length. Finding the number of words is a matter of counting the words in one line and multiplying that first by the number of lines and then by the number of pages. The number of words per double spaced, pica type page averages 270, depending, of course, on the vocabulary level.

If you are writing for children, the publisher may ask you for the grade level. There is a formula for that which was created by Richard Gunning as a way of determining the readability of a sample. It is called the Gunning-Fog Index and is an extremely useful tool. There are three steps to the formula. (1) Count out one hundred words of the sample. If it is a particularly long piece, count out several samples. End the sample nearest the sentence ending. (2) Take the average number of words per sentence and divide by the number of sentences. This will give you an average sentence length in words. Count the three syllable words - not counting proper names or easy words or those ending in "ed" or "ing". This gives you the number of "difficult words" per sentence. Take the total of the average sentence length and the number of three syllable words. (3) Divide this sum by 4. This gives you a readability level - (the grade level at which understanding can be expected). A long rambling novel suggests extraordinary printing costs and may demand special consideration. Of course, if the work is designed according to the requirements of a particular imprint, the length will already have been decided as dictated by the publisher. You can find out specific requirements from publisher's tip sheets and writer's guidelines. It is well to stick to the prescribed specifications.

The design of the book's chapter headings and section titles, should be of corresponding size and font design throughout. Additional material, such as the introduction, (a presentation of the point of view taken by the author), the preface, (the author's personal statement regarding the writing of the book), prologues, (used principally in fiction to orient the reader to the material), dedications and acknowledgements, (personal mention of the person or persons whom the author would like to thank or to honor), etc., are the responsibility of the author and need to be prepared with the same dedication and care as the main body of the book. A foreword is usually the contribution of someone other than the original author.

Fiction seldom needs back pages unless the work is an elaborate historical epoch or has some basis in fact. The requirements for non-fiction might include a bibliography, appendices, an index, references, a glossary and possibly source material lists. Epilogues are not seen very often these days, though they are used occasionally to lend a semblance of veracity to a story.

The first thing that is evaluated by the agent is the look of the presentation. By examination he decides whether the query letter is a professional petition or whether the author simply sent the entire manuscript without first determining whether it is something that the agent is willing to volunteer his time and attention to read. No matter how persuaded the author is concerning the inherent quality of his story, it is of no consequence at this stage. The author may be totally convinced that once the reader has had a chance to look over the precious material he has labored to put together, he will intuit that there is money to be made here if only one could spin the dross into gold. Then, in disregard for the amateurish qualities of the document, he will pant for representation. It does not happen that way. A submission that is haphazardly put together will only serve to turn off the agent and create an unfavorable bias for the work as soon as it comes into the office.

CAVEAT SCRIPTSIT   (Let the writer beware)

A few admonitions regarding the material: The physical nature of the submission is taken as representative of the quality throughout. An editor is apt to flip pages to see if there is a balance of dialogue and description. Long, full pages of description signal an "as told" story about.... There is a vast difference in a "story about" and a "story". The uninterrupted descriptive passages denote that the well-used axiom, "show, don't tell" has been violated. When the author goes into his "telling" mode, the reader is ignored and his reaction dismissed. It usually means that the writer does not trust his reader to understand what he has written. In its place is information concerning values and attitudes that have been placed there by a lazy writer who has intercepted the connection between the book and its readers and interpreted the actions, impressions, reactions and feelings of his characters for him. This is usually evidenced by the use of adverbs, for example, take the phrase: "She smiled willingly." A preferable description would be: "The tenseness in her body relaxed at his offer and she moved toward him, her broad smile signaling complete agreement."

Reader identification that supports and encourages involvement in the story is missing. Permitting the reader to become aware of the characters and their life struggles through seeing how they react is impossible when the author takes a teacherly posture. Messages are fine, but as one Hollywood wag once said, "If you want to send a message, use Western Union." That's still good advice. When the writer puts himself in the manuscript and interjects his observations, opinions and biases, the reader can detect it and, finding no reason to call into play his own reactions, bypasses any serious contemplation on his part. It is this interference that is the tip off that a heavy penned author has distorted the balance between action, dialogue, description and narration.

The essence of the character can be portrayed by the use of noting actions, reactions, goals, internal dialogue and memories; or the writer can take a short cut and tell his readership what to think. The practice is a dead give-away of the calibre of the narrator and a fair indication of whether professional acumen is or is not present.

Contents are crucial to the acceptance of the manuscript. Many writers in their initial projects fail to properly understand that the form of a novel is as classic as that of any other art form. Unfortunately, if a manuscript is rejected by a publisher, it more than likely will be accompanied by a form letter and the writer whose work is rejected may never come to know the reason why. Frequently the reason for rejection is because the novice will have structured his work on a linear series of events rather than on human nature. Emphasis on a time sequenced course of events is formulating the work at a level of comprehension that is too shallow for a novel. Dramatizing a chain of happenings leaves the narration flawed. By the report-like nature of its contents, the event based novel is limited to exposition, information and chronology, and, thus, devoid of emotional content. Such a story follows the organizational pattern of a newspaper or periodical feature. Event follows event. The characters are barely developed. There is no range of change within the story and the characters are ready to face the next event in the manner of a television episodic series where we expect to meet the same unchanged and unchanging people week after week ad nauseam. If your characters are no different at the end of the novel than they were at the beginning, beware. Your project will be headed for repeated rejection.

Regardless of the originality exhibited in of a piece of writing, there are genuine factors that determine its acceptance in the book stores. Ideas must be fully developed. Regardless of the novelty of the concept, when you are seeking a publisher, you must have a product which he can sell. For personal experiences without a substantial built in market - "pre-sold" is the industry term - sales are difficult if not impossible without an expensive advertising campaign and the potential for ROI (another business term. This one means return on investment). The publisher is going to be looking for a story that already has an intrinsic readership. Your chances to attract publication are much better if you are a celebrity, and even more so for one with a following. Take note: Books about Marilyn Monroe are still on the shelves years after her death.

One very special note. No matter how much enthusiasm has been awarded to the work, it is better to be objective when sending your manuscript out. Telling the publisher or the agent that you have written a very good book and he will surely like reading it does not serve to influence the professional reader at all. It is his business to make that evaluation for his company and writing to him saying that all your highly qualified friends are lavish in their praise and highly respected authors have generously endorsed it only indicates that you're hoping to buy his approval by what others think. Subtle persuasion won't work with a professional reader. It is prudent to stifle that endorsement and simply let the work speak for itself.

ALONG FOR THE RIDE

The initial presentation is different for a work of fiction than it is for non-fiction. Non-fiction is defined as that which is based in fact. For a non-fiction proposal (and proposal is the operative word here), a mission statement is essential. In the mission statement, you define the scope of the work in a thorough description of the project. The publisher will want to know numerous details: the number of pages, the number of words, whether there are graphics, charts, photos or illustrations, and is there an index and/or a glossary? If the material is potentially libelous, verification, permissions and authorizations are also needed. Do you have the proper authorization and documents? Will you need to obtain releases?

In offering a book of non-fiction, is this the writer's first bid for professional status? If so, the publisher will want to know whether you are familiar with professional procedures and can work diligently under stress of editorial demands. Is your material original and authentic? Is it factually correct? Does it qualify as professional? Does your work have broad general appeal?

There is no need for a formal registration or copyright at this point. (Under the law, unpublished material is protected until the time when it is offered for distribution or sale.) Also important is a statement regarding the significance of the topic and whether or not there is similar information readily available to the public. A strong assessment of the need for such a book goes a long way toward acceptance. A description of what is included in the form of a table of contents, with a sentence or two about what each chapter contains comes next. Include a few sample chapters and fifty or so pages (possibly the first three chapters) of actual text. If the book is non-fiction a table of contents should be included.

The biography of the author is structured like a resume, detailing writing experience that applies specifically to this project. Any formal writing that found its way into print is worth mentioning. The purpose of this is to assure the publisher that you have achieved a fair level of competency.

The fiction manuscript needs to be accompanied by a brief synopsis, a summary of the main action points of the story in chronological order; a description of the main characters and the premise of the novel, with a special notation of the features that shape its character. Indicate in your synopsis whether or not there is drama, tension or suspense and the subject around which they occur. Two to five pages in length is good.

TWICE TOLD, TWICE SOLD

It is not necessary for your book to feature an ingenious and unique concept. An original treatment of a familiar idea is perfectly appropriate. In fact, most material is derivative. After all, storytellers have explored all human relationships many times over. I am not entirely convinced that there are only thirty-six plots, as we have been told (Story Plotting Simplified, Eric Heath, The Writer, Inc.,). There are new ways for people to relate to one another and there need to be new ways of telling about them, but the major human conditions, such as the seven deadly sins which point to the primary emotions of envy, lust, sloth, anger, pride, covetousness, and gluttony have been the mainstay of literature for centuries. Remember the myth of the apple in the garden?

The adaptation of books to plays to films to musicals is commonplace. Sequels of movies use the same characters, locations, relationships and events with apologies to no one. Television sit-coms lift out characters and spin off new series. In 1993, a film, The Wide Sargosso Sea, was made from a novel written by Earnest Rhys using the character of Edward Rochester and the woman he was married to prior to his marriage to Jane Eyre in the novel written by Charlotte Brontë. The brouhaha over plagiarism is highly overrated.

COMPETITION

What about first novels? What are the chances of one being picked up by a publisher? Of first novelists who have secured five and six figure contracts, all have come highly recommended, either by a writer already under contract to the publishing house with good strong sales, or the sworn endorsement of a graduate school professor who exalts the undiscovered talent of his favorite student. It also helps if you are one of the small group of people who are highly visible, willing to hustle, who are comfortable making public appearances, agreeable to making promotional tours and appearing at book signings, sitting in on radio interviews and TV talk shows and other programs used to generate public awareness. It also helps to photograph well.

About one hundred and fifty first novels were purchased by major houses last year; one hundred and fifty out of the thousands of manuscripts competing to become one of the sixty thousand books that were eventually published. Even with my sometimes questionable arithmetic, that figures out to be one in four hundred of those brand new authors who received contracts and whose books were actually scheduled for production. All this discussion about probability is not designed to discourage a new author from pursuing the satisfaction of publication or to dissuade him from his efforts. Quite the opposite is true. It's the agent's job to worry. That's what he is there for. If there is a message here, it is for the individual author to persevere. These figures only prove that good material is hard to find, so don't be discouraged! First novels <u>do</u> get published and it can happen to you!

ONE HUNDRED THOUSAND COPIES

Bestseller lists are created by several different entities. The New York Times has a weekly list. USA Today has a list. Not all lists draw from the same source. Though they are not identical, one thing is obvious. A cursory inspection will show that the novels on anybody's bestseller list are authored by writers with familiar names who have already established a reliable readership. Nothing sells like fantastic sales records. Success with earlier editions is a strong motivation for the publisher to open wide his pocketbook for advertising and marketing to ancillary markets. Keep your eye on the doughnut not the hole. Keep thinking about those one hundred and fifty first novels that made it. They, too, started out with a first sentence.

What's the next step if you are seeking publication? During the process of trying to interest a publishing house in your project, you might discover that the one house you have set your eyes on will only accept manuscripts submitted by an agent. That sometimes happens. It simply means that you will have to restructure your marketing plan.

The first requirement before submitting to anyone is to make the book as good as you possibly can. Take a second look at what you have to offer. Look at whatever similar work is available for purchase. The manuscript needs to be readable and it helps if it is topical, exciting and innovative.

Having a track record of publication is a definite plus when it comes time to submit. Any writing experience is valuable. If you have been a reporter on a high school paper or a local newspaper, don't be afraid to list that. If you have written advertising copy, that's definitely worth mentioning.

If you have absolutely no writing experience, there are a few alternate ways to qualify. Writing with a well established collaborator is one way. Of course, it means being able to find someone who is willing to share the work and the rewards with you, but if you are determined to break into print and do not have any credits, it has been done. If you are writing a non-fiction book and you have been associated with a high profile in the field, you might try getting the person to write an introduction. Undoubtedly, publication without professional status is a tougher way to go. It pays to persevere. Everyone who ever got published had to start somewhere. Someone had to take a chance with them.

A little tip. If your book is non-fiction, you might find a specialist in your field to create a forward for you. It always helps to have a recognizable authority whose opinion is recognized lend a boost to your project by way of recognition and introduction. Of course, you will have to supply a copy of the manuscript for the expert's use. Include the information regarding the endorsement in the presentation proposal you send out to an agent or a publisher. You need not send the entire forward, but mention can be made of the background and standing of the particular specialist who has lent his name to your book.

Of course, having chapters of your book published in periodicals is another. Entering writing contests is an excellent way to bring your work to the attention of an agent or a publisher. Remember, like taking olives from the jar, the first one is the most difficult, but after that one is out of the way, it's a lot easier. Use your creativity on yourself and your career. Stay with it. Remember: Publishers cater to special markets and are just as individualized as the readers they serve. You only need one. A good match of author and publishing house is what it takes to get the story sold.

Chapter Ten
****

THE AGENT

agent \'a-jənt\ n [ME, fr. ML agent-, agens, fr. L, prp of agere to drive, lead, act, do; akin to ON aka to travel in a vehicle, GO again to drive, lead] (15c) 1. a: something that produces or is capable of producing an effect : an active principle 2 : one who acts for or in the place of another by authority from him: as **a**: a representative, emissary, or official of a government <crown~> <federal ~> **b :** one engaged in undercover activities... **3 :** a means or instrument by which a guiding intelligence achieves a result.
- Webster's Ninth Collegiate

Well, I guess that's enough An agent is the person who stands at the gateway to fulfillment of your dreams.....

You're convinced that your manuscript is as good as you can possibly make it Friends and relatives have given it their approval. What's the next step? You'd really like to see your book out there in the book stores. You've sent it out to a few publishers, but they have sent it back to you with nothing but a form letter The business of rejection is hard enough without getting the courtesy of a personal response. One or two of the publishers you sent your manuscript to wouldn't even look at it. You're thinking it has been a waste of time to try to do it yourself. Maybe you don't know the right people? Maybe you need an agent?

You've heard that getting an agent is like getting a loan. You can get one if you don't need one, but how can you fulfill your dreams of becoming a high profile professional without one? It's time to get ready to make the leap from amateur to professional. Time to get the answers to the catch twenty-two that every writer faces.

LOOKING FOR MR. GOODWRITE

Literary agents work under the same set of unwritten rules that guide the publishers, distributors, reviewers and store owners All are dependent upon the response of the reading public for the success of their industry and are guided by the choices in reading matter made by the buying public. Depending upon sales to generate his income, a literary agent's success is in direct proportion to the sales of his clients. Placed in the position of giving freely of their time and only receiving fees when they can market their client's work, agents are forced to be objective and pragmatic. To assure their ongoing success, they sell to the circle of book publishers with whom they have prior experience, those who have been helpful in promoting the work of their clients. In larger agencies or publishing companies, there will be entire departments delegated exclusively to one specific genre. As a result, the reader, the editor and the department may have established a tradition of working together. It is to this team that the author brings his manuscript.

Let me describe what it is like from the receiving end. You can imagine since our agency accepts queries from beginning writers, we go through a lot of unsolicited submissions. It is a thrill for an agent to discover someone with talent and we definitely enjoy finding and working with a writer who shows promise. When the query comes in over transom, it is put aside until such time as it can be given our undivided attention. Sometimes that takes a couple of weeks, but it guarantees that the manuscript will get serious consideration. The packet is slipped out of its jacket and the contents are inspected.

The cover letter is read to discover what skills the author has demonstrated. Naturally, poor language, grammar and syntax count against our acceptance. We look at format. From the letter we are able to get an impression of what the author feels about his work. We know if the letter is frivolous or hostile, that the person is not going to work out well. We consider prior experience and the reason for writing the material. If that is all within the range of acceptability, we read the synopsis for style and content. If, after reading the synopsis and weighing it with the cover letter and the writing experience of the author, we find that the novel has merit, it is then that the left brain goes to work and our experience comes into play. We do not like reading about gratuitous violence so we have made a rule that we do not consider it for representation. We have no objection to most other types of material which could possibly contain literary values. Marketability is judged somewhat on subject matter, but mostly on quality. Length of the manuscript has no value either way, though if less than one hundred pages, it is considered short.

Frequently, we will get inquiries about an idea for a book. We then reply that ideas are not our stock in trade and must be fully developed before being considered. Personal experience stories are evaluated on an individual basis. Of course, celebrity and "tell all, tall tales" are popular right now with the proper marketing plan. I should say here that originality is not as impressive as style. So called "new" stories can only be based on changes in politics, sociology, and psychology. Romeo and Juliet has a few thousand versions to go yet, before it becomes outmoded. After all, Casablanca featured two lovers from hostile ideologies. The conclusion should be obvious -- you can't argue with success.

The potential for publication is weighed against all factors and a decision is made whether or not the project is one in which we will wish to become involved. If the prospect seems favorable that our office and the author will be able to work amicably together, an invitation is extended to submit the entire work. If the author shows promise, but has not already had publication experience, he will be offered the opportunity to work with a professional reader who will extend guidance through the evaluation process until such time as the work is ready for submission to a publisher. The success of that process depends largely on the cooperation of the author.

If the applicant has sent us an entire manuscript to read, the inquiry is put aside until a fuller reading can be assigned. If the assessment comes back favorable, the same opportunity will be extended and an agreement form is sent out.

Once in a while, an author will say "Just send it out over your name... I'm not interested in taking lessons". The agent's reputation is on the line with each piece he sends out. It is just not feasible for our agency to act as a conduit through which unexamined writings are funneled.

When the material is sent in, the process then focuses on the professional reader who has been selected for compatibility and enthusiasm for the subject matter. He goes over the material with a helpful attitude and a blue pencil, just as a publisher's editor would do. From this procedure he is able to prepare a complete evaluation. This document, a copy of which is forwarded to the author, enables us to determine whether it is appropriate to consider representation at this time. Once an author has worked with an editor, that editor stays with the writer until such time as the project is ready.

The evaluation by the reader is not a vague subjective exercise. It is based on many qualitative elements. It starts with flipping pages. From this preliminary scanning, the balance of dialogue to narration is noted. Such elements as length of scene can be easily determined from the briefest and most casual inspection. Within the first few pages, it is possible to tell whether the author has made a good start. The editor looks to see if he can identify the subject matter immediately and whether it is presented in a lively and provocative manner. If the beginning is filled with background explanations and history, it tells something about the writer's skills. Is the main character presented in a sympathetic and interesting manner? Are the events secondary to the humanistic considerations? Does it have emotional content? Does the style fit the text? Does it play out in present time or is it etched in historical stone? Is the structure proper for the progression?

In our consultation services, the agency provides a comprehensive evaluation consisting in rating the elements of the manuscript. All documents are gone over for style, language and format. Non-fiction is compared to work of the same genre in book stores (or libraries) and a ranking is given. It is examined for a fresh point of view or a new concept. In fiction such components as characterization, structure, conflict and resolution are graded and if we feel that changes will help the piece, specific suggestions are made to formulate a more acceptable manuscript. If the agent is truly interested in proposing representation, a request for rewrites may be made.

If editing is needed, it will be suggested to the author that it is advisable although, as a rule, this is not suggested until a final draft is ready. That way, duplication and unnecessary work is avoided. If the writer agrees, the service is provided for him. Technical elements are checked for accuracy. Once the client and agent reach a consensus on the text, it is reviewed for appropriateness. The potential market is interpreted and targeted.

The agent weighs the biographical material that he has on his author and works with him to formulate the best presentation he can. Experience that counts towards assembling a creditable resume is any track record with the demands of publishing. Working with a well established collaborator reflects favorably on one's reputation. Any excepts that have been published in periodicals; articles, and/or reviews, or any prize winning material is worth mentioning. All references make the job of the agent easier.

If the book is non-fiction, a proposal is developed at this point. The execution is a very specialized production. It is the tool that is used to determine the feasibility of publication. It consists in a review of the subject, a mission statement, a table of contents and a synopsis of each chapter.

As soon as the author and agent have endorsed an agreement, the agent begins providing services to his client. The manuscript is put into appropriate format. The biography may be customized for a particular targeted market. The most significant service he provides is access to the publications market. This is a highly cultivated skill depending upon associations made by the agent. Photocopies are made and the manuscript is prepared for mailing. Current knowledge about what a publisher is looking for guides the agent in his search. Phone calls verify the agent's plans. According to what the agent knows about the publisher's needs and the client's objectives, he is able to make wise choices in matching efforts. By keeping up with current trends, the agent passes on the trends he discovers in book buying to the author, who relies on his advisor's impressions for rewrites and editorial decisions. The agent, by offering the submission over his name, verifies the quality of the book and screens the work for the publisher. It avoids that horrible unopened rejection and may even merit valuable feedback.

Preliminary talks are begun. An offer is made for the book. The agent evaluates the terms and if they are not standard or do not represent favorable clauses, negotiations take place. All this happens without the participation of the author/client, although he will be notified that talks are taking place.

When a suitable offer is made and terms are agreed upon, the client is notified. The agent guides the author through the contract terms. If he is agreeable, the sale is made and the book now belongs to the publisher. With certain contracts, approval of the author is required for publishing decisions.

Arrangements are made for the degree of marketing participation by the author. Subsequently, the agent monitors and evaluates contract performance. He handles money, keeps records, and issues drafts.

On the occasion when the publisher makes suggestions regarding ways to improve the marketability of the work, the client makes his decision with the guidance of his agent. While the stock in trade of the literary agent is his knowledge of the marketplace, he has several other quality services. He is a professional and a specialist in all areas of writing. Using a literary consultation service is the best method of finding a collaborator or ghost writer. From his experience with the writer's capabilities, he is able to judge the experience levels of his writer's skills and match them to the task. He is good at matching the capabilities of a collaborative arrangement paring styles, temperaments, and interests. The agent can contract for and assign work for those authors whose work is familiar to him. Any agent who has been in business any length of time has a roster of professional writers. He can evaluate the ghost writer's efficiency in meeting deadlines and rewriting. He knows what is going on in publishing.

It is inadvisable to send a complete manuscript to an agent without querying him first. Expecting he will take time from his other writers to involve himself in working on a uninvited script is assuming that he has little to do. He earns his living by selling -- not by reading all the unsolicited novels he is invited to read. It may be a perfectly wonderful piece of writing -- even the best he has ever seen, -- but it starts the relationship off on a bad foot. Make his job easy. Read his guidelines as published in the Writer's Marketplace. He will be happier if you follow them and he will be more willing to work with you than if you ask for special consideration.

Now that you know what an agent can do for you and you have decided to find your very own, how do you go about finding one? If you have been writing for a while, you will know some editors and writers working in the field. Ask them whom they suggest. They will probably be glad to give you a recommendation. They might even arrange an introduction. If you have attended a seminar or lecture, you may have heard a lecture by a presenter who is willing to look at your material. Social or professional contacts may be able to help.

If you do not have any personal resources to tap into, occasionally, the forward or dedication of a book may mention the name of the agent involved in its sale. Look up agencies in the library - Writer's Market, Literary Market Place, Writer's Yellow Pages, California Writers and Publishers, and (In Europe) The Writer's Handbook and Writers' and Artists' Yearbook. In New York City there is the Society of Author's Representatives, (local - NY) and the Independent Literary Agent's Association, all of which have rosters you can send for.

Writers' groups may have recommendations of literary agencies. Local adult education schools have these professionals on their teaching staff. Writer's groups sometimes keep rosters and someone in one of the groups may have had experience with one and can make a recommendation.

For those authors who are writing screenplays, the process is a little bit different. Major studios will not accept unagented material. The Writer's Guild of America regulates and limits the activities of writers applying for recognition in the entertainment industry. There is a more viable opportunity with smaller independent companies which are usually a better bet for unsold writers whose reputation does not precede them. You can purchase a register of production companies active in the industry. For the names of these companies, check the annual issue of the Hollywood Reporter (published in October) or the Oscar issue (in April), or, if the time of the year is not right, the Thursday issue every week will give the names, addresses, staff positions and phone numbers of companies which have films in production. Each company is formed for a particular picture so don't write the production company. Address your query to the producer.

Finding the agent who is a perfect match for you requires some degree of organization. Narrow down to your targeted agency from the listings in the Writer's Market. Study the requirements of the most likely companies to determine the match of the agency to your material. Find the name of the agency which will accept your manuscript . You now have an idea of where to apply. You have classified your book and targeted your agency. It is an easy step from that point to then select a half dozen or more agencies to which you have decided to apply.

Organizing the search is easy. Prepare a book in which to record your progress. Across the top of the page (sideways) place the following headings:
- i Title
- ii Agency
- iii Phone number
- iv Editor
- v Call made/date
- vi Sent out
- vii Postage
- viii Date returned
- ix Comments (rare)
- x Ac'pt/Rej

Get the name of the agent to whom you will be sending your submission. If you are not certain of the person who will eventually read your manuscript, call the agency and ask. It may be appropriate to ask to speak to him. Tell him what you have and ask if he will read it. Prepare your cover letter and address it to him directly. Send your sample, if it is a non-fiction book, send the complete formal book proposal. If it is fiction, send a synopsis, about three chapters or about fifty pages.

A photocopy is permissible if it is of good quality. Multiple submissions are acceptable provided the manuscript is developed according to strict professional format. Once you have put it in the mail, wait a reasonable period of time for a response. It may take weeks or even a couple of months to get an answer. In this instance, no news is certainly good news. The obviously unacceptable manuscript is generally returned immediately. Being unperturbed and patiently conditioned to waiting for the reader's reply is a good attitude to cultivate. It will come in handy. (When your book is slated for printing, it will take upwards of a year before it is in the book stores, so be resigned to letting others set the pace.) You've done your work well. The rest is up to fate, timing, the publisher's advertising budget and the vagaries of public taste.

Chapter Eleven

****

WHAT TO DO 'TIL THE SCRIPT DOCTOR COMES

> A good many young writers make the mistake of enclosing a stamped self-addressed envelope, big enough for the manuscript to come back in. This is too much of a temptation to the editor.
> - Ring Lardner

There are as many reasons for a manuscript being turned down as there are for its acceptance. While there is no one single error that clearly stands out as the reason why the majority of books are refused publication, in the years that I have been submitting manuscripts to publishers, there are a few oversights that writers make that crop up regularly. Without knowing what they are the author becomes vulnerable to rejection and subject to frustration and discouragement. Eliminating possible grounds for a rebuff will increase the chances of possible success. The necessary information is not readily available. You can learn about it, though, through extensive experience with a broad range of genres and classifications, through guidance from a knowledgeable friend or associate, or in a book like this one where the entire process is outlined.

THE "R" WORD

The reasons for rejection vary with each publishing house. If the pairing of the book with the publisher does not come to pass, it may quite possibly be a problem that can be remedied by persistence and diligence. When the mismatching of the work and the publishing house occurs because the book doesn't meet the requirements of the publisher's list, it does not reflect unfavorably on the quality of the work and further efforts conceivably will pay off.

One practice of the industry is the manner in which rejections are handled. Notification of the rejection accompanying the returned manuscript is invariably a pre-printed rejection form letter leaving the author disappointed and confounded.

Some of the reasons why a publisher will reject an otherwise acceptable book are because selection requires unanimous approval of the entire staff which the submission did not receive. The fledgling book may have been beaten out a competitive submission. It may be that the timing of the offering is off. I know one author who waited five years after his script's first submission before it was purchased. To persist in the submission effort demands unshakable confidence on the part of the author that his book is of professional calibre and that there is an probable market for it.

Another reason for a publishing house refusal originating with the book's editors is because they may already have purchased a book that addresses that same topic, or perhaps they may feel that a particular author is the wrong one for that book. Alternately, the publishers may already have someone under contract creating a similar work. They may even have already produced a comparable manuscript for their list. Another cause for turning down the opportunity to purchase an original manuscript might be because the capital outlay and necessary personnel required to publicize the work may already be committed to another project.

Under these conditions, it is not the failure of the material that is the cause of rejection. If this is the case, more care needs to be taken with the applications to see that they are sent to where they will be more favorably received.

When all the conventions of submission have been carefully observed and the manuscript continues to be rejected, there are several reasons that might account for its lack of success in finding a publisher.

If the writer is convinced that the manuscript holds promise despite the failure of the process, he may opt to continue with submissions for a while. How long the author continues to submit his project depends upon the project and the author. There is no set time limit. I have known manuscripts to be accepted after a year of continuous submissions. Sir William Golding, author of the now classic novel "Lord of the Flies", had his work rejected by twenty-one publishers. On the twenty-second submission, it was accepted.

Failing to obtain acceptance and being unwilling to delay publication for such a long period of time, an author can always resort to self-publication. It is an interesting process and under these circumstances, one that should not be overlooked.

There is more competition in non-fiction and it is more subjective. For this reason is more difficult to get published. Established criteria must be met just the same, but timeliness, which is important in non-fiction is not as crucial in fiction. For this reason a manuscript that may be well written may be passed over.

Language that is inappropriate to its readership is promptly rejected. Stories targeted for the youth market using a collegiate vocabulary are obviously inappropriate. Literature for the children's market needs to be aimed at the selected age level. Care must be taken to grade the content and style. The number and character of illustrations should be considered as well. I have found librarians in the children's section to be quite knowledgeable regarding a child's ability to handle language and subject matter and can offer invaluable information. An excellent reference for subject matter is the Stith Thompson Motif/Index classification. Another is the Storyteller's Source Book. Whatever grade level is chosen, mismatches between the intended reader and the content is especially critical. Avoid flowery language, archaic or little used words. Clarity has a high value in any type of writing. Computer software, such as Grammat-ik, include style and grammar. The Gunning-Fox Index and the Flesch-Kincaid formula are useful for gauging readability.

Works of fiction are rejected for numerous reasons, the most widespread cause lies in the technique of the writing. Signal flags go up indicating certain errors are present. Naturally, grammar, syntax and punctuation faults weigh heavily against acceptance. Repelled by material rife with violations of writing rules and principles, the reader/editor suspects that the author is not well schooled, careless, or at worst, indifferent. All of the professionals who deal with original creative material receive stacks of novels in every mail. If the spelling in one is poor, there is hesitation to delve into the story line. If the story is marginal, poor language skills will tip the scales against it. Technical factors weigh heavily in the first impression.

It is very important when considering fiction to keep in mind that drama is conflict and the more levels involved, the better. Idyllic fantasy is fine for daydreams, but not for fiction. The admonition to use conflict does not equate with violence. Conflict in story structure refers to three major sources: man (generic) against man, man against nature and man against himself. Without opposition, man cannot be measured. It is in facing his demons that the best in man is manifest: courage, selflessness, risk, forgiveness, high principle, and altruism.

Additional matters of style that will cause a novel to be rejected lie in the way the story is told. Starting the story too early and taking several pages to introduce the main character before launching into the main story line is one mistake made often. It demonstrates that the writer lacks control over his material. Use of numerous flashbacks is another. They stop the story's forward movement waiting for background information to be revealed. This slows the narration.

One very subtle and serious flaw that marks the amateur is the practice of dramatizing a chronology. A favorite mechanism is to construct and defend a plot line because it really happened. The beauty of fiction is that it has a structure, makes sense and has closure, -- a quality that is lacking in life and one of the charms found in reading. In storytelling, a work of fiction can introduce the reader to unfamiliar lifestyles. An author can create themes of justice and reward, love everlasting and grateful children. Literature is a boon to man and has the ability to enlighten and to satisfy like no other medium. Why copy life?

Authors new at fiction writing will write a sequence of events in dialogue form. This type of writing is flat. There is a vast difference between reporting, (though it is structured in drama form) and rendering, using the all the available techniques of novel writing. This error occurs when the author emphasizes events as played out in the manner of a newspaper report, or, as Sergeant Friday used to say, "Just the facts, Ma'am."

Richer, more rounded stories are told using the characters' point of view with descriptions, impressions and attitudes coming from the characters rather than the author. Writing that presents the author's impressions rather than those of his characters' is a dead give away. The key to spotting this style error is the author's generous use of adverbs.

A first time novelist is wise to use the third person limited point of view until such time as he has mastered it. First person point of view is more dynamic in certain genres, like detective novels, but without expert handling, the POV tends to get preachy and stiff. Restricting the writing to the first person voice limits perception of what has transpired to that of his personal knowledge. This variation of the narrative voice is apt to get the inexperienced writer in a bind. He may find that his main character needs to know something that he has not witnessed and without it, the story crashes. Third person limited is much easier to expound than the first person POV which takes advanced skill to use properly.

A story needs to have a well-defined beginning, middle and end and it needs to meet the rules of story structure which are: what happens when a person has a problem and needs to solve it. The content is better when the character endures a range of emotion during the process and at the conclusion undergoes a profound change. Without change in the main character, the material is episodic. This point alone is the cause of more rejections than any other element of fiction.

If the author is willing to work and rework his material when a manuscript's rejection is due to an inherent weakness, it can usually be made better. I can guarantee that the way to improve that first effort is to write a second and a third.

There is always a valid reason for a book being rejected, though the veto seems to the writer to be unfair. The causes for rejection are many, but they need never be considered final. Discounting refusals resulting from a book having been sent to an inappropriate publishing house, rejections based solely on the quality of the material can benefit from being reworked.

Taking all these factors into consideration, most rejected writing can be helped by a rewrite. Remember. Writing is rewriting. When a book is selected for publication, it is because the subject, the style, the name of the author, the excellence of the writing and the appropriate nature of the material all come together with a great match of book and publisher spiced by incredible timing. A lack of any one of those elements is apt to result in a refusal. Sounds like luck has a lot to do with it, and it does, but only after all the other requirements are met.

If the author is ready to become a professional and all else fails, consider that this is a new career and if building that career means having to start small with submissions to periodicals, newspapers and corporate house organs, do it. Rejection only means that you have not persisted in cultivating your skills enough to have attracted the right publisher - - YET.

GLOSSARY

Advance - The sum the publisher offers pre-publication.

Antagonist - The character opposite the main character who provides the principle conflict.

Author's copies - Usually less than twenty volumes but the publisher may offer to sell additional publications at a discount.

Back matter - That which is included in the book in back of the main body of information.

Backlist - enjoy modest but steady sales over a number of years. The "bread and butter" of the publishing industry and the goal of the author looking for ongoing income.

Berne Convention - The document that controls the ownership of authors off shore.

Catalog - the publishers inventory of books in print.

Categories - Genres of literary effort. Western, gothic romance, sports, religion, women's studies, Most category fiction is published in paperback.

Common law - applies to that which belongs to the public heritage (fair use), i.e., the dictionary, the history of man, geographical places, ideas.

Conflict - Opposing forces, the basis of all drama. "Must" vs. "Cannot". Protagonist vs. Antagonist. The very essence of drama, tension and suspense.

Copy edit: The practice of checking facts for accuracy - not typographical errors or misspelling, grammar or punctuation.

Copyright - establishment of the date of completion as registered with the government agency.

DBA - Doing business as: A pseudonym.

Dot matrix - A class of printer in general use acceptable for submissions.

Epiphany - The pivotal point in a story when a significant realization is formed frequently leading to the resolution.

Fair Use - The use of literary material for which no permission is needed when in the service of study, research, review, newspaper criticism, summary comments, determined by 1) purpose and character of the material, 2) the amount in proportion to total, and 3) the effect of the use on the market.

Fax - Most printers have faxes that are capable of receiving information from anywhere and can be transmitted to you. If you send original material via electronic transmission, be certain to include a disclaimer to protect the ownership of the material.

Front list - current publications

Fiction - created from the imagination, not true.

Galley - the first printed format of the book.

Genre - classification given a work of fiction for ease in thinking about the material and grouping it with similar works. i.e., romance, action/adventure, horror, sci-fi, fantasy, detective, etc., All have sub-genres.
Guidelines - Publisher's requirements.

Hard Copy - computer generated paper copies.

Imprint - One of the companies under the umbrella of a parent publishing company.

Indemnity - Security against hurt, loss or damage. Responsibility for.

Information Superhighway - The process of obtaining available information through the use of computers.

Juvenile - directed toward young people

Libel - That literary crime that consists in slanderous material in print.

Line editor - minor smoothing out of the transitions, tightening sentences, etc.,

Line -An imprint within a publishing house.

Lists - a publisher's inventory of the books he offers. Spring list. Fall list. Also an indication of the types of books he accepts.

Literary property - an entity that has ownership quality.

Midlist - those books whose authors may have missed the best seller list the first time out, but the new publication of which has stimulated sales on previously written books and now are responsible for a steady trickle of copies from season to season.

Multiple submission - circulating several copies at the same time.

Nom de plume - a name used in lieu of the genuine another name - a pseudonym.

Non-fiction - Factual, informational, biographical, how-to, true crime, expose, true stories, academic, research, social commentary, -- based on material that is not created from imagination.

Novella - Long story or short novel 7,000 - 15,000 words.

Originals - a term used by paperback publishers to identify books first published by pb houses.

Packagers - former editors or former members of the publishing industry who develop ideas, hire authors and contact publishers to propose books. Also called "book producers".

Peripty - The turn around in the story, the twist that brings about the defeat of the antagonist.

Proofs - a preliminary print out of a manuscript for which it is the obligation of the author to revise and/or edit material as requested by the publisher.

Protagonist - The main character, the one around whom the action occurs.

Pseudonyms - Using another name than your own. If you select another name for your authorship, remember that you may need to have an additional checking account, etc.,. Can be created by the use of a D.B.A..

Public domain - Material that is not under protection, such as: words in the dictionary, the history of man, geographical locations, items of common heritage, and ideas.

Reader - A professional in the agency or publishing house who is the first person to receive the manuscript.

Registration - Process by which the date of completion is recorded for motion pictures by the writer's guild.

Remainders - Overstock or returns that are sold at discount and/or mail order.

Reprints - Secondary sales, i.e., paperback

Rewrite - A normal process of creative writing. It some-times is requested by an agent or publisher.

Roman à clef - A novel in which the real persons or actual events are portrayed in disguise.

Seasons - Spring and fall, the period when new books are introduced to the public along with the new list. Most publishing houses have semi-annual sales conferences.

Secondary markets - Non book store locations which handle book sales. (Ex. Sporting goods stores, health food stores, etc.,)

Sequel - A second manuscript using the same time frame, the same persons, places and/or incidents as the original. Considered a special class (not necessarily treated as an original work). The production of the derived book can be contracted for or assigned.

Slush Pile - The popular name for unsolicited manuscripts. It is a good practice to address your inquiry to the editor who will in all probability read your manuscript. If a submission is undirected, it will likely come back to you with a form letter rejection.

Subgenre - divisions of genres, i.e., Harlequin Romance: Historical, Presents, Regency, Temptation, Superromance, Intrigue, American Romance, all having their own guidelines.

Subsidiary rights - videos, toys, T-shirts, mugs, cartoons, songs, etc., Rights are marketable away from original material.

Subsidy publisher - a publisher who charges the author for typesetting, printing and promoting his book.

Tip sheet - The guidelines put out by the publisher reporting exactly what he is looking for in the way of new material.

Title - a term meaning number of books - We are publishing so many titles this season.

Trade book - "Trade" in most industries means "of or to the trade." In publishing, "trade" (also called general books) means just the opposite - books sold to the general public....

Trade size - (trim size) Dimensions of a book. 5 1/2" x 8 12/2"; 6" x 9"; oversize, 9" x 12"; and mass market paperbacks 4 1/4" x 7".

Warranty - That which is declared to be true. A promise.

Vanity Press - Publication which charges the author for the service - see Subsidy publisher.

1099 - the tax form that is used to report income from creative work.

APPENDIX

Appendix - 1

SUBMISSIONS FORMAT

1. Legible, Typewritten/computer generated
2. One side of paper only
3. Use white, good bond paper (20#)
4. Double spaced
5. 1" margins all around
6. Pages should be numbered:
    a. Upper right, or bottom middle.
    b. Alternate: author's name and page number on upper right
7. Fiction/Non-fiction - unbound
8. Give number of pages for sample and total for completed manuscript
9. Movie scripts - bound
10. Title page
    a. Title
    b. Author's name and address
    c. Registration or Copyright
    d. Date or draft number

Appendix - 2

WHAT TO INCLUDE IN A PROPOSAL FOR A NON-FICTION BOOK

1. The overview: Subject hook: make 'em drool for it in one hot page quote, an event, an idea or a joke, anecdote or statistic that rivets the editor's attention.

2. Title and subtitle. Can you refer to it with two or three words by subject? i.e., "Bicycling for Fun"

3. Selling handle - A sentence or two that can be used for promotion.

4. Length - A good length is 60,000 wds or 230 pages unless the topic is technical or breakthrough.

5. Book's other features: Tone, (humorous, serious, down-to earth), Exercises? Charts? Additional attributes of your book?

6. The identification of a well-known authority who has agreed to write an introduction to the book. (Suggestion - 500 words)

7. A sentence about what you have done to prevent possible technical and legal problems. Check for libel, privacy rights, copyright infringement.

8. State if it is a multiple submission.

9. Back Matter: Appendix, notes glossary, bibliography, index.

10. Suggested markets for the book. What kind and how many? Statistics on sales of same subject books, magazines or merchandising TV, media, events.

11. Subsidiary rights if any. Newspaper or magazine brief excerpts.

12. Possible spin offs, ancillary marketing,... (sweatshirts, notebooks, mugs, posters)

13. Who will review the book?

14. What you will do to help promote the book? Write magazine articles, appear on PR circuit, lecture, give seminars. Can you produce a following of people who know of your work?

15. The names of books that will compete with and compliment yours.

16. Resources needed to complete the book:
    a. Time for research
    b. Additional financing
    c. Artwork, photography, an introduction, creating an index, research for accessing data
    d. Permissions to use quotes. (Number only)
    e. Less than 250 words okay.

Appendix - 3

CHECKLIST FOR FICTION SUBMISSIONS

1. Be sure you are familiar with the type of manuscripts currently being published by your target publisher.

2. Manuscripts must be typewritten on standard sized paper (8 1/2" x 11"), white paper, double spaced, on one side of the paper.

3. Do not submit a carbon copy. Computer NLQ okay.

4. Be sure to keep a copy for yourself, manuscripts do occasionally get lost in the mail.

5. Include a self-addressed, stamped envelope large enough to hold your manuscript should it need to be returned. Please include a large enough envelope for a response. Do not send cash. Use checks, money orders or stamp coupons.

6. The accepted length for a novel manuscript is between 60,000 and 100,000 words (approximately 200 - 400 manuscript pages).

7. Most publishers prefer to see only the first three chapters (@50 pages) and a complete synopsis rather than the complete manuscript. If they want to see the entire work, they will request it.

8. Please indicate if you are creating multiple submissions. Some publishers do not accept them.

9. Allow at least 90 days for a reply; after three months you might politely inquire as to the status of your submission.

10. Publishers do not want to see complete submissions. Please do not send disk, fax, or on-line submismission without express permission. They will not be read.

Appendix - 4

SAMPLE COVER LETTER

Jimmy L. Writer
4242 Fortunate Street
Lucky Hollow, NO, xxxxxx

This date

Editor
Company
Bonanza Rd.
Big City, NY xxxxx

Dear Editor:

    I enjoyed speaking with you by phone on Tuesday. When we talked I mentioned the manuscript, (name of), which I am enclosing.

    (Something about the project - why he should read it, how long it took to write, some interesting thing about your motivation.)

    My qualifications are -- and I have a background in...

    My writing experience - (if you have none, speak about what sorts of things you like to read.)

    (Similar books in the book stores.)

    I would like you to consider this book for publication by (company name).

Yours sincerely,

Appendix - 5

PROOF MARKS AND CORRECTIONS

ab	Ambiguous	Mix	Mixed construction
ad	Incorrect use of adverb or adjective	Sub	Faulty subordinate clause
agr	Agreement error	Ref	Reference unclear
Big W	Big words	Trite	Trite expression
Cap	Use capital letter	SL	Sentence length
No Cap	No capital letter	Sp	Spelling
lc	Lower case	≡	Capitalize Name
case	Wrong pronoun case	Mod	Misused modifier
?	Is this okay?	T	Tense
DM	Dangling modifier	O Pn	Omit punctuation
F	Fragmented sentence	Inc ¶	Inconsistent para
FS	Fused sentence	Sl	Slang
GE	Grammatical error	ST	Stilted language
Id	Idiomatic	Start	Start here
Log	Error in logic	F Sp	Figure of speech
Mng	Meaning not clear	Inf	Phrase too informal
MS	Error in manuscript form	∽	Order should be transposed
N u	Nonstandard usage	WW	Wrong word

Org	Organization fault	W	Wordy
Pass	Ineffective use of passive voice	Var.	Sentence variety
⊙	Period	abr.	Abbreviation
?	Question mark	sp #	Spell out numbers
;	Omit semi-colon	/	Separate words
∧	Comma	⏎⏋	Indent paragraph
,	Omit comma	→	Bring to mark
!	Omit exclamation point	¶	Begin new paragraph
:	Omit Colon	∧∨	Equalize spaces
/--/	Dash	#	Insert space
( )	Parentheses	∧	Insert letter
∧∧	Quotation marks	w.f.	Wrong font
[/]	Brackets	b.f.	Bold face
/.../	Ellipses	stet	Let stand
/=/	Hyphen	⌢	Transpose Letters
ℓ	Take out letter	No ∧	Comma fault
⌒	Close up	—	Delete words
⌊	Move line left	u.c.	Upper Case
⌋	Move line right	→|	Check margin
out	Something missing	FL	Foreign language
spell out	Spell it out	+	Center
Ital	Use italics	/0	Size type (number)

Appendix - 6

Getting Permission: A letter must be prepared to request permission to use charts, graphics and original art work:

Your Address
City State Zip
Date

Corporate representative, title
Corporation
Address
City State, Zip

Dear (Company rep):
    I am currently preparing a .... with the working title of .... being published by or, I have not secured a publisher as yet. I have completed a draft of the manuscript and I am writing to you to secure permission to reprint the following:
                1.
                2.
I am enclosing photocopies of each.
    I request permission to reprint these items in this and all future editions and revisions. I also request worldwide rights in all language and handicapped media editions. Full credit will, of course, be provided. Please specify the desired credit working to be used for credit lines or citations.
    For your convenience, a release statement is provided below. A duplicate of this letter is also enclosed. Upon your approval of this material, please sign both copies and return one to me in the self addressed, stamped envelope. Please retain a copy for yourself as well as the photocopied figures.
    Thank you so much for your time and consideration. If you have any questions or concerns at all regarding this request, please contact me at 1-(818) 508-6296 either voice or fax on any working day between 9:00 AM and evening.
    I look forward to your reply.

Sincerely,

Permission is granted to use this stated materials as outlined above.
Signature: Title:
Date:

Appendix - 7

RESOURCE ADDRESSES

Writer's Market Writer's
Writer's Digest Books
Department JA
1507 Dana Avenue
Cincinnatti, OH 45207

Artist's Yearbook
A & C Black Ltd
35 Bedford Row
London WC1R 4JH
United Kingdom

Literary Marketplace
R. R. Bowker
245 West 17th Street
New York, N. Y. 10011

The Writer's Handbook
45 Islington Park
London N1 1QB UK
European and American

The Writer's Yellow Pages
P. O. Box 190831
Steve Davis Publishing
Dallas, TX 75219

Romantic Times
163 Joralemon St. Ste1234C
Brooklyn Heights, NY
11201

Author's Guild
234 W. 44th St.
New York, NY 10036

National Writer's Club
1450 Havana, Ste 620
Aurora, Co 80012

Mystery Writers of America
17 E. 47th St 6th Fl
New York, NY 10017

Western Writers of America
P. O. Box 823
Sheridan, WY 82801

Science Fiction Writers
of America
P. O. Box 4335
Spartanburg, S.C. 29305-4335

Writer's Guild of America West,
Inc.
8955 Beverly Boulevard
Los Angeles, CA 90048
Guild Member Signatories

Appendix - 8

ITEMS IN AN AUTHOR/PUBLISHER CONTRACT

1. The name of the author (and any pseudonym) and the title of the work

2. Its length in number of words

3. When and in what condition it is to be delivered

4. In whose name copyright is to be registered

5. The publisher's exclusive and nonexclusive territories

6. The advance against royalties if there is to be one

7. The royalties to be paid (on the retail price of the book or "actual cash received")

8. A listing of the ancillary sales for which there will be adjusted royalties

9. The subsidiary rights granted the publisher (such as book club and quotation rights)

10. The division of earnings between author and publisher from these rights

11. The author's warranty that the book is original or belonging to the author

12. Affirmation that no comparable or competitive work will be produced

13. Warranty that the work contains no libel or invasion of privacy of another person or other unlawful matters

14. Agreement by the author that he has obtained written permission for any copyrighted material

15. When and how often statements and payments are to be rendered by the publisher

16. The time period the publisher has within which he must publish the book or lose the right to do so

17. How many free copies the author will receive

18. At what discount may the author buy additional copies

19. Rights of first refusal for the publisher

20. The penalties if the author fails to deliver a final manuscript or it is unacceptable to the publisher

21. Provisions for termination (and reversion of rights) if the book goes out of print

INDEX

"2001", 68

A
Advance, 31
Advertising, 10
Agency,
 roster, 52
Agent, 7
 associates, 138
 finding one, 102
 Finding, 23, 95, 133
 finding, 139
 percentage, 94
Agent's
 agreement, 137
 reputation, 135
 responsibility, 138
 submission evaluation, 136
Agreement form, 135
Asimov, Issac, 70
Association meetings, 33
Author,
 bestselling, 8
 Need, 25
 Profits for, 17
 publisher considers, 17
Author, experienced,
 qualify as, 74
Author's,
 biographical material, 137
 biography, 137
 impressions, 149
Authority,
 Literary expression, 19
Authorization,
 permission, 38
Autobiographies, 6
Autobiography,
 candidate for, 20

B
Back cover,
 copy for, 9
Back pages,
 need for, 122
Bank account, 36
Bedtime story, 44
Berkley Publishing Group, 13
Bestsellers, 129
 creation of, 73
Biographies, 6
 authorization, 49
Biography,
 author's, 127
Blanchard, Kenneth, Ph.D.,
 One Minute Manager, 13
Bolles, Richard Nelson,
 What Color Is Your
 Parachute, 13
Book clubs, 39
Book producers, 115
Book proposal, 20
 non-fiction, 137
Book publication,
 Requirements, 24
Book reviews, 10
Book store owner,
 Profits for, 17
Business-like atmosphere, 22

C
California Writers and
 Publishers, 140
Capote, Truman,
 In Cold Blood 53, 68, 70
Career,
 writing, 39
Cartland, Barbara, 40, 42, 70

Casablanca, 135
Chandler, Raymond, 70
Chapter headings, 9
Character,
    creation of, 51
    range of change, 149
Characteristics,
    Writers, 22
Charts, 9, 38
Children's books 6
Children's literature, 52
Christie, Agatha, 70
Clancy, Tom,
    The Hunt For Red October 53
Classic form, 45
Classifications,
    books, 54
Clerks,
    book store, 96
Client's objectives, 138
Collaboration,
    advantages, 26
Collaborator, 20, 26
    Working habits of, 26
Collaborators, 21
Common Law Property, 82
Community interest, 20
Computer generated data, 11
Computer software, 147
Concept,
    original, 71
Conflict,
    importance of, in fiction, 148
Consultation services, 136
Contests,
    participation in, 27
Contract,
    pre-publication, 20
    reporting, 32
Contracts
    six figure, 29
Contracts,
    book, 94

Cookbooks, 6
    popularity of, 52
Copyright, 9, 127
    fourteen classes of, 79
    how to obtain, 83
    transfer of, 86
    unpublished works, 81
Copyright Act, 78
Copyright notice, 82
Copyright registration,
    eligibility for, 80
Copyright, international, 85
Correspondence schools, 39
Courses, 7
Cover, 9
Cover letter, 134
Credits,
    Acquiring, 21
    building, 33

D

Dances With Wolves, 54
DBA (doing business as),
    securing, 35
Deadline, 40
Dell Publishing, 104
Designer,
    Profits for, 17
Desk top publishing, 11
Detective stories, 68
Diagrams, 38
Dialogue, 58
Discipline, 32
Distributor,
    Profits for, 17
    securing, 12
Dramas,
    need for copyright, 82
Dramatic elements, 47
Drawings,
    need for copyright, 82

E
Editing,
  need for, 137
Editor, 8
Expenses,
  in-home office, 36

F
Fair use doctrine, 38
Fiction,
  category, 51
  classifications, 67
  contents, 57
  fact content, 50
  fashions in, 68
  style of, 148
First novels, 128
  annual, 18
  publishers and, 72
  purchased, 72
First refusal, 115
Flashbacks,
  use of, 148
Fonts,
  suitable, 9
Form letter,
  rejection, 8
Format,
  submission, publisher, 93
Frances, Dick, 23, 70
Fulfillment house, 106
  rental, 10

G
Genre,
  requirements, 66
  types, 48
Ghost writer, 20, 21
  offer, 7
Golding, Sir William,
  "Lord of the Flies" 146
Gram-mat-ik, 147
Gunning Fog Index, 147

H
Harcourt, Brace,
  Jovanovich, 104
Harlequin, 104
Health and beauty, 6
Hillerman, Tony, 68
Hollywood Reporter, 140
How-to's, 6
Humor, 6
Hunt For Red October, 68

I
Idea, good, 7
Ideas,
  marketability, 57
Illustrations, 9, 38
Imprints, 47, 104
Incorporation, 36
Independent
  Literary Agent's
  Association, 140
Index, 9
Information super highway 77
Inspiration, 22
  Holding, 23
Intellectual properties,
  ownership of, 77
Intellectual property,
  registration for, 78
ISBN (International Standard
  Book Number), 9
ISBN,
  meaning of the numbers, 88
  securing, 88

J
Johnson, Spenser, M.D., .
  One Minute Manager, 13
Journalist,
  career, 41

K
King, Stephen, 23, 53, 70

L
L'Amour, Louis, 23, 53
Language early 43
Language,
    need for, 44
Lawyer,
    As representatives, 25
    entertainment, 72
    Fee scales, 25
Lectures, 7
Legal profession,
    publishing involvement, 20
Libraries, 39
Library of Congress card number,
    obtaining, 90
Library of Congress number, 10
Library resources, 140
List, 105
Literary agency, 21
Literary agents,
    fees, 133
    inquiries to, 134
    methods of, 133
    services, 139
Literary consultant, 16
Literary ideas,
    theft of, 37
Literary Market Place, 140
Literature,
    feminist, 53
    gay and lesbian, 53
Ludlum, Robert, 23

M
Mainstream novels, 6
Mankiewicz, Joseph L., 6
Manuscript,
    classification, 60
    length of, 135
    potential, 54
    research, 7
Manuscript submission,
    numbers game, 98

Market,
    importance of, 66
Marketing plan, 65
Market research, 64
Mentor, 18, 25
    academic, 8
Mission statement, 137
Monroe, Marilyn,
    biographies, 68
Motion pictures,
    need for copyright, 82
Motivation, 29
    amateur, professional, 62
Multiple submissions, 142
Musical compositions,
    need for copyright, 82

N
Name,
    ownership, 34
    rights to, 35
Narratives,
    event driven, 50
Negotiations,
    timing of, 138
New Age, 6
New literary voice, 18
Non-fiction,
    criteria, 69
    proposal presentation, 126
Notoriety, publishers
    Seek out, 20
Novel,
    non fiction, 53
Novelists,
    first, 7
Novels, 46
    contents, 48
    mainstream, 52

O
Objectivity,
    need for, 97

Office of Copyright, 81
Originality, 37
    myth of, 128, 135
Ownership,
    laws, violation of, 87

P

Page numbering, 121
Paperback writer, 41
Paperback, publishers, 47
PC disks, 11
Pen name, 34
    collaborators, 34
    ghost writers and, 34
Performance,
    showcase, 56
Periodicals, 39
Personal experience, 6, 57
Photographs,
    need for copyright, 82
Pictures, 38
Plagiarism,
    definition, 38
Plays,
    legitimate stage, 46
Point of view,
    third person limited, 149
Popular demand,
    creation of, 17
Popular media 45
Popular media,
    in the 90's, 45
PR,
    Author participation, 17
    campaign, 100
Printer,
    hired, 10
    Profits for, 17
Professional author,
    definition, 75
Professional career,
    qualifying, 22
Professional reader, 136

Professional reading,
    for objectivity, 59
Professional status,
    first bid, 55
Professionalism,
    Acquiring, 22
Professor,
    Recommendation, value of, 26
Publication,
    chances for, 61
    motive for, 12
Publisher, 7
    financial risk, 10
    need, 25
    staff, 109
Publisher's needs, 138
Publisher's Weekly,
    sales data, 95
Publishers,
    financials, 112
    size of, 104
Publishing agreements, 116
Publishing companies,
    sales force, 114
Publishing house,
    major, 9
    presitigious, 8
    selection, 93
Publishing procedure, 112
Publishing trends, 99
Publishing,
    risks, 64

Q

Query,
    agent, 139
Quotes,
    use of, 38

R

Reader,
    as arbiter, 63
Readership, 17

Reading public,
  preferences of, 23
Record keeping, 30
Records, 32, 97
Rejection letters, 98
Rejection,
  process, 145
  unknown causes, 143
Rejections, 149
  handling of, 145
Release,
  need for, 70
Remainders, 23, 30, 64
Reporting or rendering,
  differences, 148
Representation,
  self, 91
Representatives,
  overseas, 10
Resume,
  author's, 130
Returns, 30
Reward,
  financial 29
Rewrites, 7, 137, 149
Romance novel,
  sales leader, 68
Romance novels, 6
Romeo and Juliet, 135
Royalties, 23, 31

S
Sales,
  campaigns, 111
Santmyer, Helen,
  And The Ladies of
    The Club 40
Sci-fi, 6
Screenplays, 140
Sculptural works,
  need for copyright, 82
Secondary markets, 63
  copyright considerations, 88
Self help texts, 6
Self-publishing, 9, 12
  new standards, 11
  process, 106
  requirements, 105
Self-representation,
  pros and cons, 99
Selling, 22
Seminars, 7, 40
Seven deadly sins, 128
Sheldon, Sydney, 23, 70
Simon and Schuster, 104
Slug lines and headings, 122
Small press,
  advantages of, 105
Society of Author's
  Representatives, 140
Statutory copyright,
  definition, 82
  length of, 85
stick-to-it-tiveness,
  value of, 19
Steele, Danielle, 22
Storage facility,
  rented, 10
Story, 17
  beginning, middle
    and end, 5, 149
Story rights,
  sale of, 72
Storytelling, 6, 22, 43, 148
Style and content, 17
Submission,
  appearance, 119
  length 121
  process, 97, 101
  tone, 124
Subsidy houses,
  president, 10
Subsidy press, 12
Subtitle, 9
Superhighway
  information, 82

Superhigway
  electronic, 77
Synopsis, 127, 134, 137
System of payment, 30

T
Table of contents, 9, 137
Talk shows, 12
Targeted readership, 14
Taxes, 34
Ten Speed Press, 13
Terminator, series, 68
The Unforgiven, 54
Themes, 148
  finding, 58
Time Publishing Group, 104
Tip sheets, 66, 104
Title page, 120
Trade journals,
  advertizing in, 12
Trade magazine,
  subscription, 33
True crime, 6, 68
True Life story,
  style, 70

U
Use of adverbs, 149

V
Vanity press,
  expense, 12
Vidal Gore,
  Burr, Washington, D.C.,
  Lincoln, Empire, 1776,
  Hollywood, 53
Violence, 148
Voice, 58
  finding your, 58

W
Warner Books, 104

Westerns,
  in film, 54
Work place, 32
Works of Art,
  need for copyright, 82
Workshops, 40
Writer,
  character, 18
  creative, 16
Writer's Guild of America 6, 56, 140
Writer's Handbook, 140
Writer's Market, 92, 140, 141
Writer's Yellow Pages, 140
Writer-for-hire,
  assignments, 56
Writers
  Charaterisitics, 19
Writers' and Artists' Yearbook, 140
Writers' conference, 18
Writers' groups, 42
Writers-for-hire, 114

A Writer's Guide to making the transition from writing for fun...to writing AS A CAREER MOVE...

SAVE AT LEAST TWO YEARS IN YOUR SEARCH FOR PUBLICATION.

* How to format your submission
* How to write a query letter that will sell your work
* Understanding the language used by professionals
* How to avoid falling into the "slush pile"
* Organizing the search for a publisher
* Where to submit
* Coping with Copyright procedures
* What to expect from an agent
* What the publishing business is really like
* Finding the right person to help you

Get all the help you need to make the leap from struggling artist to published author in one comprehensive source. Learn from a teacher and consultant who has taught others how.

Please send me_____copies of DO THE WRITE THING: MAKING THE TRANSITION TO PROFESSIONAL at $18.95 each plus $2.00 for shipping and handling)

I am enclosing $ _____

Send check or money order, no C.O.D.'s please. Make check payable to:
      Myriad Press
      12535 Chandler Blvd #3
      N. Hollywood CA 91607-1934

Name_____

Address_____

City_____State_____Zip_____